HOW TO SUCCEED AS A

ENTREPRENEUR

Running a Business without Letting It Run Your Life

GARY SCHINE

Dearborn™
Trade Publishing
A **Kaplan Professional** Company

This publication is designed to provide accurate and authoritative information in regard to the subject matter covered. It is sold with the understanding that the publisher is not engaged in rendering legal, accounting, or other professional service. If legal advice or other expert assistance is required, the services of a competent professional should be sought.

Vice President and Publisher: Cynthia A. Zigmund
Senior Project Editor: Trey Thoelcke
Interior Design: Lucy Jenkins
Cover Design: Design Solutions
Typesetting: Elizabeth Pitts

Published by Dearborn Trade Publishing, a Kaplan Professional Company

Printed in the United States of America

03 04 05 10 9 8 7 6 5 4 3 2 1

Library of Congress Cataloging-in-Publication Data

Schine, Gary L.
How to succeed as a lifestyle entrepreneur / Gary Schine.
p. cm.
Includes index.
ISBN 0-7931-6418-4 (6 × 9 pbk)
1. New business enterprises—Management. 2. Vocational interests. 3. Entrepreneurship—Psychological aspects. 4. Small business—Management. 5. Success in business. I. Title.
HD62.5.S3523 2003
658.1′141—dc21

2003000919

Dearborn Trade books are available at special quantity discounts to use for sales promotions, employee premiums, or educational purposes. Please call our special sales department, to order or for more information, at 800-621-9621, ext. 4404, or write to Dearborn Financial Publishing, 30 South Wacker Drive, Suite 2500, Chicago, IL 60606-7481.

Dedication

Dedicated to my wife, Ellen, for persuading me that this needed writing and that I could write it.

C O N T E N T S

PREFACE

Why I Wrote This Book

After I finished college in the mid-1970s, I began work for New York University (NYU) as a video production specialist. Eventually, I was promoted to an administrative position overseeing video operations for NYU's School of Education. While at NYU, I also did a fair amount of freelance video work. I didn't love being an administrator nor did I love that all my time was taken up by work. I was married now and wanted to spend more time with my new wife. I also didn't love feeling that the demands of my job seemed to be stripping me of my personality and replacing it with the personality expected of a young college administrator. In the late 1970s, I decided to concentrate on my freelance video work and leave my day job.

The freelance work I was getting when I was at NYU provided a nice extra income in addition to my regular paycheck, but it wasn't enough for survival without that paycheck. I figured that with more time to devote to freelancing, I would get a lot more work—but I figured wrong. I decided that my difficulties as a freelancer were a result of my lack of business knowledge (I think I figured right on this one). To remedy that lack, I enrolled in an MBA program with the idea of putting the knowledge I'd gain from a business degree to work in running my video business and thus allow me time with my family and for other things I wanted to do.

Very few of my business school classmates had aspirations that were in any way similar to mine. With no more than one or two exceptions, they were relying on the MBA degree as a ticket to a major corporation job that would lead to promotions and corporate management, not to any type of self-employment or small business career. Few of my classmates seemed to give any thought to lifestyle needs or even to the line of business of their future employer. If a job offer came through with a good salary and decent prospects for promotion, the prospective employer's function wasn't important, nor was its location, nor the hours it required, nor even the responsibilities of the job itself. The goal was clear: a management job with promising prospects for promotion.

This pervasive attitude baffled me. Didn't anyone else care about what they actually did on the job for 40 to 80 hours a week? Didn't they care whether they would be working in Hartford or Los Angeles, or even whether in a metropolitan or rural area? Didn't it matter whether the company where they would spend most of their waking hours and all their work efforts was manufacturing food additives or publishing books? The answer was no.

Though my classmates were not very much concerned with the content of their job or their lifestyle freedom, I knew that many self-employed people *were* concerned with these elements of their life. Friends who were running video companies would think it ludicrous if someone were to suggest they consider running a meat packing company instead regardless of increased income. Friends in other fields they loved would think it equally ludicrous if someone suggested they leave their field for another that offered more rapid promotion. And at least one friend who runs a shop in Greenwich Village would throw me out of her shop if I suggested she relocate it to . . . well, anywhere really . . . just to increase her sales. It became clear to me that these self-employed people needed to learn business tools and how they could employ those tools more creatively and meaningfully than a lot of my business school classmates could. In a vague sort of way, I decided that maybe some day I would write a book for these lifestyle entrepreneurs.

Well, I got my MBA, and I did put it to work in a video business that I started with a partner in 1980; the business was successful but a bit frustrating. It became more about money than about self-expression and creativity, and it wasn't the most efficient way for me to make money. I gradually lost sight of my own lifestyle goals and eventually left the video business in hopes of a more lucrative way to use my MBA skills. The idea of brokering businesses seemed like a good one (that is to say, a potentially lucrative one), so I started a company to do just that. I almost forgot about the book idea and even about my dismay with my classmates who didn't consider their lifestyle needs along with their career. Perhaps I was becoming more accepting of their attitude.

Although it took nearly ten years for me to lose sight of my lifestyle goals, it took me only a moment to gain it back. That moment happened in August 1989, when my doctor told me I had incurable cancer and a limited amount of time to live. Immediately, my thinking changed from work and career to my family—which by now included not only my wife but also two young children—and to how I would spend the rest of my finite life. I'm not the first person to observe how well a life-threatening diagnosis shows its recipient what is truly important.

I resolved then and there that family, lifestyle, and making a unique contribution to the world (two if I could live long enough) were my priorities. Work would be a way to enable those ends; they would not be ends in themselves. But first I had a little obstacle to overcome: my incurable leukemia. I solved that impediment by finding a new treatment my doctor should have known about but didn't. That's a story in itself that I related in a book I wrote about finding and using medical information (first published as *If the President Had Cancer,* later revised and republished as *Cancer Cure: How to Find and Get the Best There Is).*

I was cured of my incurable cancer (as I write this, I'm more than 11 years cancer free) thanks to an experimental treatment that was administered to me at Scripps Clinic in La Jolla, California, in early 1990. My cancer experience and the book I wrote also offered me the opportunity to make one contribution to the world—and to do it through a small business. I started Schine Online Services to help others with serious illnesses search for new treatment possibilities. That business has been quite successful both as a business venture and, more important, as a service that has not only saved several lives but has taught many clients about innovative treatments.

I remembered recently that when I received my cancer diagnosis, I resolved to make two contributions (not just one) if I were to live long enough. I also remembered the book I resolved to write so many years ago while I was an MBA student. Here is the book. I hope you'll agree that it is at least a modest contribution to those who want to use small business to attain a well-considered life.

CHAPTER

1

A Different Sort of Entrepreneur

My sister is a successful entrepreneur. But you won't find stories about her business successes in the *Wall Street Journal.* For that matter, you probably won't find her reading the *Wall Street Journal* or any other business publication. Bobbie probably couldn't explain the difference between a stock and a bond and doesn't know about—or care about—the prime rate or the latest analysis of policies of the Federal Reserve. She doesn't know much about accounting methodologies, mergers and acquisitions, or techniques of modern management. She's not even rich.

How then is she a successful entrepreneur? Bobbie is a *lifestyle entrepreneur.* She uses the tools of business to live life on her own terms. After college, she learned karate and fell in love with the sport. She also became active in the then fledgling women's movement. So she combined her love of karate and commitment to the women's movement into a business: a karate school that taught only women. Bobbie works roughly half-time. You see, besides karate she loves a lot of other things and sees her work as a means of supporting a lifestyle, not as an end in itself. She's successful in having made her love of karate her work and, at the same time, carefully integrating the rest of her life with her work. The rest of her life includes long annual trips to Guatemala, working with cancer patients, and spending time with friends. Her business is a vehicle to living the lifestyle she wants to live.

My friend Sam (some of the names used in this book have been changed to protect individual privacy) is also a lifestyle entrepreneur but one unlike Bobbie. An expert in preserving the architectural and historical integrity of religious structures, he is highly trained and highly skilled in this field. Sam's credentials include a Ph.D. degree and numerous publications in professional journals. Even though his consulting work takes him to all parts of the country and beyond, finding those consulting assignments has been and continues to be a challenge. Many professionals are equally well qualified and well versed in numerous off-the-beaten-path fields. Like Sam, many of these professionals want to turn their professional skills into their own small business but find doing so a challenge.

Finally, my friend Richard was diagnosed with aggressive lymphoma when he was 30 years old. His doctors didn't expect him to live much beyond his 32nd birthday, but Richard beat the odds, beat the cancer, and survived. He decided that the insights he gained from his cancer battle could help him help others who were dealing with serious illnesses. So he left a successful journalism career to offer inspirational lectures—performances really—to cancer patients and the physicians and nurses who care for them. Richard understands that he must run his performance business like a . . . well, like a business . . . to survive financially. This book is designed for people like Bobbie, Sam, and Richard.

It is for those with skills and talents who want to market their skills and talents but may be denied a ready channel to do so, either because their skills are unique or because their skills have traditionally fit into a large institutional structure, not a small business structure. It is for people who worked to become expert in a field because they wanted to, not because it was a traditionally lucrative one filled with ready opportunity. It is for those who want to use their skills to make a unique contribution to the world and utilize a small business as the vehicle to make that contribution possible. In short, it is for those who want to use their skills to design their own lifestyle. Small business provides a unique and powerful vehicle to do just that.

Any number of books are available and any number of business professionals ready to give advice to beginning entrepreneurs. Most of these books and advisors you'll find, however, just "don't get it" about pursuing unusual fields or businesses designed around a chosen lifestyle. In fact, the traditional view of entrepreneurship assumes that money making is the sole goal; even the vehicle for building the business (the day-to-day work) is secondary to the goal. If marketing cranberries looks to be more profitable than drawing caricatures, then cranberries it is.

This book explains how you can set up a business and run it on your own terms. It shows where traditional business advice does and does not apply to the aspiring nontraditional entrepreneur. Certain business tools and practices are the same whether one is starting a convenience store or a business specializing in entertaining cancer patients. Others have to be modified to apply to the artist, karate teacher, or other providers of less common services to whom this book is addressed.

Business is not an end in itself for the lifestyle entrepreneur. Rather, it is a means to an end. The end may be making a decent living while doing what you love, helping the world (or some small part of it) through practicing your skills and services, or designing a lifestyle that grants you freedom to pursue interests other than work.

ENTREPRENEUR PROFILE

Lifestyle Businesses and Eskimos

Some lifestyle entrepreneurs, paradoxically, claim to have little interest in business but view the tools of business as merely skills they need to survive economically while living their chosen nonconventional lifestyle. Sharon, one of my business school classmates, was a former VISTA (Volunteers in

Service to America) volunteer who worked with Eskimos in northern Alaska. She felt these Eskimos were slowly but surely being forced to abandon their way of life because they lacked the business skills needed to trade and otherwise survive in a world that was unconcerned with their culture. Her whole purpose in gaining an MBA degree was to return to Alaska so she could teach business skills to these Eskimos as survival skills to protect their culture and enable them to successfully coexist in a world dominated by a free market economy.

Most people who seek MBA degrees intend and expect to work for big companies and climb traditional career ladders; a few intend to start their own companies, and a few others plan to take over family businesses. When I asked Sharon about her unusual goal of teaching business skills to Eskimos, this was her response:

> Before coming back to school, I was a VISTA volunteer assigned to help the Eskimos in Alaska. I learned two things in VISTA. I learned firsthand about government inefficiency. Very little meaningful help was reaching the Eskimos despite the resources going into VISTA. Another thing I learned was that the way of life of the Eskimo is being threatened, not because they don't get enough government aid but because they don't have the basic tools of business at their disposal. They need to learn about marketing and finance and general business procedures to trade with the outside world and to survive as a culture. That's the kind of help I want to give; that's what I want to do with the business skills that I'm learning. That's why I'm taking my degree and moving to northern Alaska.

Sharon viewed business not merely as a method to live one's own chosen lifestyle but as a pathway to preserve the lifestyles of an entire culture. Her goals for business may have been ambitious, but they weren't ridiculous. Doubtless the continuation of an ancient culture is dependent on many things, one of which is economics; and the tools of business can help the economic well-being of groups of any size. Few would include business as one of the helping professions, but Sharon would, and I would too in cases like this one.

The tools of business are powerful, but they need not be the exclusive property of businesspeople any more than computers are the exclusive province of computer programmers. I intend to show how powerful business tools can be harnessed and used by anyone who wants to pursue a field of interest and a purposefully chosen lifestyle. True, most of the people who understand and use these tools do so to build traditional businesses that assume 12-hour days and a business-centered life where what they do all day is less relevant than the financial return it produces. But these same tools can help you pursue your dreams, even if those dreams are not to start the next IBM but to live life flexibly—on your own terms doing the work you want to do.

Finally, I show how you can market your services no matter how unusual they may be. Practitioners in many fields are frustrated because they can't find enough clients or find themselves working in a field other than the one for which they are trained. This is a shame, because it is easier today than ever before to successfully market unusual skills and products. It's a matter of taking advantage of the tools of business and the modern technology that is readily available and affordable.

I'll start by defining and contrasting the traditional and the lifestyle entrepreneur.

The Traditional Entrepreneur

The primary purpose of a business is to make money, preferably lots of it. This is the traditional view of entrepreneurship and the view held by many small business owners. The money is the essential goal and an end in itself. The specific business that the traditional entrepreneur enters is primarily a means to that end. The efficiency with which that particular business meets the goal of wealth is the prime, if not the only, yardstick by which the quality of the business venture is measured. The only other major consideration in determining whether a business venture is viable and appropriate is the level of risk entailed and whether that level of risk justifies the expected return. Many successful entrepreneurs in fact own several unrelated businesses and start or acquire new ones based largely (if not entirely) on their potential return on investment balanced against the perceived risk.

Most of the advice you'll hear about starting a business, including most of the books on the subject, assume that businesses are started for making money first and foremost. It's practically a truism that entrepreneurs must work much harder and for many more hours than they would for a boss. In fact, it is a badge of honor for most entrepreneurs to work 15-hour-plus days and be labeled a "workaholic." The money and the perceived status money brings are reward enough for the long hours and the risk entailed. The expensive auto and other material symbols of wealth demonstrate success, at least on this one dimension.

Nothing is wrong with this approach to small business. It has been the incentive for many bright and creative entrepreneurs to start companies that have contributed a great deal to our economy and our well-being in myriad ways. However, it is not the sole reason that people choose self-employment or set up their own business or practice. In fact, more people start businesses or practices today for lifestyle reasons than for financial reasons.

A study published by Babson College titled "Frontiers of Entrepreneurship Research" (Arthur M. Blank Center for Entrepreneurship, Babson College, 2000) reports that nearly 50 percent of those starting companies gave lifestyle reasons as their primary motivation (broadly categorized as *need for personal development* or *need for independence*). Only 16 percent said that making money was their primary reason for going into business.

Similarly, a 1999 Lou Harris survey of 1,000 self-employed Americans and small entrepreneurs ("Why We Labor: 'American Dream' Alive and Well," *PR Newswire,* 1999) found that money was not their top motivator. Nine out of ten respondents said that "setting their own priorities and independence influenced their decision most" to go out on their own.

The fact that lifestyle choice and not money is the main reason entrepreneurs become entrepreneurs is barely dealt with by those who write books on small business or otherwise dispense small business advice.

Because the tools of business are so powerful and can be applied to multidimensional ends, using them for financial ends only is selling them short. Business tools and principles, although very useful for earning money, can also be used to achieve life successes on a number of additional dimensions that are at least equally valuable to many entrepreneurs and aspiring entrepreneurs.

The tools of business, when used properly, can bring you lifestyle freedom. They can help you practice your chosen profession in a manner you deem appropriate for your own desired lifestyle. In fact, they can enable you to practice a profession that doesn't yet have an established structure for private practice. The tools of business can even help you make your chosen unique contribution to the world through your career.

The remainder of this book describes these business tools and explains how they can be appropriately adapted to the needs of the lifestyle entrepreneur. It shows where traditional advice can be readily applied to the lifestyle business, where it can be modified and then applied, and where it should be discarded. Finally, I present inspiring examples of entrepreneurs who have used the tools of business creatively to make possible well-considered lives on their own terms.

The Lifestyle Entrepreneur

The lifestyle entrepreneur can be anyone who wants to spend the career portion of his or her life doing something that doesn't fit neatly into a current job or any other job likely to be available. The unwanted restrictiveness can be as straightforward as the number of hours the job demands or the inflexibility of work schedules. It can also be the job function itself, because no organization is looking for an employee to practice the skill the employee wants to practice, at least in the way the employee wants to.

Based on my observation and on the research I've seen (some of it noted in the section above), most people who choose entrepreneurship do so to gain independence. That independence can take the form of time flexibility, job structure flexibility, or often just the freedom of not answering to a boss.

In the eyes of many, however, small business takes away one's freedom rather than allowing it. After all, according to conventional thinking, it demands hours of one's time, far more hours than a job demands. Besides time, it often demands risking money, which often means straining one's finances and financial security, even jeopardizing one's ability to acquire the goods and services that make life easier.

Paradoxically, though, a small business and self-employment practiced creatively can free some of us from careers (and by extension lives) that we deem compromising and restrictive. In reality, many people use a small business as the vehicle by which to live the life they want to live, creatively express their identity, and make unique contributions to the world. Seldom does working for someone else allow, let alone encourage, people to put their own lifestyle or self-expression needs first. But if you're on your own, you decide the priorities, and you can make your own needs—not those of your boss or the company for which you work—priority number one. Reasons that lifestyle entrepreneurs give for leaving a job and going out on their own are discussed in the following sections.

Practicing One's Profession on One's Own Terms

Typically, a prospective lifestyle entrepreneur is highly educated and/or highly skilled, though frustrated because he or she wants to do other things with that training. For example, many college professors are lifestyle entrepreneurs, privately practicing their chosen field on a part-time basis. Many more college professors want to do this than the ones who actually do it.

A number of writers who have either jobs that don't involve writing or jobs that involve writing what they are told to write aspire to be freelance writers. Through freelance writing they can largely control their work schedule and at least partly control what it is they write. Similarly, a number of artists who may work for ad agencies or for large companies aspire to do their own art in the way that fits *their* lifestyle. There are librarians who think about offering research services commercially, teachers who want to be private tutors or consultants, chefs who want to own their own restaurants, and so on.

ENTREPRENEUR PROFILE

Tenure Track versus Self-Employment

Brenda Rosen and my wife have been friends since graduate school days. Brenda was working on a degree in education and my wife on one in psychology; both received their Ph.D. at the same time.

A few years later, they got together for lunch. Brenda told Ellen about conferences she was attending and papers she was presenting at those conferences. She was also complaining that despite the many talks she was giving, she still hadn't received a tenure-track academic appointment.

Ellen asked her how much she really wanted that kind of academic appointment. Brenda, who apparently hadn't considered this question before, didn't have a ready answer, and in fact didn't seem to quite understand the question. Ellen then said, "You know, you already have your degree, so there is no need to present papers unless you want to, or if doing it provides a means to a goal you want to achieve. There are other things you can do with your degree." Brenda was speechless, apparently in the midst of what psychologists call an "aha" moment. It had never occurred to her before that a career path didn't have to be linear—college, graduate school, academic appointment, tenure.

Brenda realized that an academic job wasn't really her goal; she just assumed that was the next step. In fact, she realized her *inner entrepreneur* (I don't think psychologists use this term). Brenda Rosen, Ph.D., now has a business (which she prefers to call a practice) assisting the parents of academically gifted children to set up appropriate educational plans for their children. She negotiates with schools, arranges private tutoring, and even persuades college professors to allow kids as young as 14 to take their college-level classes.

Brenda essentially markets her practice by contacting school guidance counselors for referrals of students who fit the gifted criteria. Most guidance counselors are happy to give her referrals, because most schools are at a loss in dealing with students who are academically years ahead of their peers. If an outsider can help, they're delighted.

Brenda couldn't be happier with her career as a self-employed person. She talks a lot about the "little geniuses" she deals with and the reactions of college professors to these kids who do college-level work before they reach puberty. She got a call from one of those professors recently: "Remember how you talked me into accepting that 15-year-old boy into my computer science course by assuring me he would keep up with the class? Well, the class just ended and his performance was far from the class norm." Brenda feared she had made a blunder this time until he continued. "He did so much better than anyone else in the class, finishing with an average of 108, whereas the second highest average in class was 91." I'm not sure where she'll send this boy next, but I'm sure she'll figure something out.

Brenda hasn't taught a college class or presented an academic paper since her aha moment 12 years ago.

Organizational Culture versus One's Personality

It's often not the work itself that aspiring entrepreneurs find distasteful but rather the structure of a job that doesn't allow asserting one's personality. It may well be a matter of feeling as though you are abdicating your personality to fit the corporate or organizational image. Those who do happily fit into organizational cultures probably would have difficulty understanding how the issue of being a misfit can be so important to some people. Complaints about dress code and other corporate policies seem to be whining and nitpicking. But the whole is more than the sum of its parts to those who feel it's just *not them.* They can explain that they don't like to wear a tie, suppress their political views, or require the boss's approval for vacation dates. To most people these are, at worst, minor annoyances; they understand and accept that such policies are essential to maintain the corporate image and organizational order. To some—many of those to whom this book is addressed—they are threats to their individuality and their very happiness.

Many people, in fact, look to corporations or other organizations to provide them an identity more important than the one they have on their own (I'm not just John Doe; I'm John Doe, vice president of ABC Bank.). They look at the organizational structure as a benefit and fitting into that structure as a noble pursuit. Climbing the organizational chart is challenging and successes in the climb meaningful. Others, those who have probably had difficulty fitting in from the time they were children, continue to have difficulty abdicating their personalities to the organization. Some of these people look to their own business as a way to create an entity reflecting their own personality and interests rather than the other way around.

Making a Unique Contribution through One's Own Business

Some people go off on their own because they have an overriding need to make a unique contribution to the world. My friend Richard, who left a career in journalism to help cancer patients, fits this profile.

If you own the business, you decide its priorities. Although maximizing the owner's income is the traditional top priority of most small businesses, it doesn't have to be. As long as income is adequate to meet the expenses of the business and its owner, other priorities are possible. If you want to help the world and use your business to do it, there is no reason not to pursue your altruistic goals.

ENTREPRENEUR PROFILE

Does a Job Have to Be Traditional to Be Real?

David Vernaglia graduated from Brown University in 1992 with a degree in classics, which he studied for the sake of learning and continues to study for the same reason. Though his degree qualified him to teach either Latin or ancient Greek, he knew the market for both was limited, but he still hoped to teach one day. Dave looked for a teaching job with no luck, so he accepted a customer service job with AT&T. To say he was ready for a change after two years there would be an understatement. When he was offered the chance to teach two courses at a private school, he accepted the job, even though the pay was ridiculously low. He figured the job might be a stepping stone to a full-time teaching job one day.

After a few months, Dave received a call from a parent asking if he would tutor her child in Latin; and then a similar call came from another . . . and another. He became fascinated with the then nascent World Wide Web and learned to create Web sites and network computers. Soon he started getting calls asking if he would be interested in putting together a Web site or helping with a networking problem.

Dave grew up in a family in which both his parents were full-time teachers; and his older brother was a CPA working for a large accounting firm. Entrepreneurship was not a family tradition, so it never occurred to Dave that he could work on his own and on his own terms. But with teaching a couple of Latin classes, tutoring Latin, and the computer-related jobs, he was very much a self-employed lifestyle entrepreneur, though he didn't define himself as such. Dave figured that all this was a stopgap until he could find a "real" job with a "real" boss.

But he loved his "stopgap" lifestyle. He had lots of time to garden, study Latin, travel, and do the other things he wanted to do; all it took was mental reframing. Dave soon realized that his stopgap activities added up to a very nice career as a self-employed worker. After all, he had the time and schedule flexibility to pursue his other interests, and he was making a lot more money than AT&T was paying him. "Why," he asked himself, "do I want a traditional job? A job can be a real job even if it's not a traditional job. Does a job have to be separate from the rest of your life in order to be real?" His family doesn't understand his thinking; they still think of it as a stopgap until he lands that real job.

Dave called me a few days ago to say he had just completed a three-week networking job. Though he had to work 21 very long days in a row, the job paid about as much as AT&T was paying him for a full year of being whined at and generally abused by customers. I think his lifestyle business is going far too well for him to think about a "real job" right now, and I think Dave agrees with me.

ENTREPRENEUR PROFILE

Schine Online Services

Permit me the indulgence of using myself as an example of a lifestyle entrepreneur.

In 1990, I was diagnosed with a rare form of leukemia and was told by the diagnosing oncologist that I had from a few months to several years to live, but he was clear that there was no cure for my condition. Well, I decided to learn what I could about this enemy that was going to kill me and apparently had every chance of success.

A few days into my research, I learned about a new treatment for hairy cell leukemia that was in clinical trial in California. Though the article I found in the venerable *New England Journal of Medicine* was published three months before my diagnosis, my doctor had no knowledge of this new treatment. The article reported only about the 12 people who had been treated to date, 11 of whom were in complete remission.

Six months later, I was on a plane to California to get this new treatment. Three weeks after arriving, I was on my way back home to Rhode Island, a bit weakened by the arduous treatment but free of cancer I hoped. Several months later, I seemed to be cured of my "incurable" leukemia, a state of health that continues to this day, now more than 11 years later.

For the first year following treatment, I was haunted by the fact that my local doctor had had no knowledge of this treatment, despite the fact that it appeared in the premier journal of his field, the *New England Journal of Medicine.* What's more, I learned that my situation wasn't unique; doctors are not always aware of the latest development in treatment, and people die because of it. I had to do something with this information to help others learn what their treatment options might be.

I wrote a book titled *If the President Had Cancer* (later retitled *Cancer Cure: How to Find and Get the Best There Is* by the publisher). The book stresses the need for patients to become fully informed about their illness and explains how to go about doing that. I also started Schine Online Services, a service business whereby I search for treatment options and developments for any illness suffered by my clients. Rather unexpectedly, the business got a great deal of publicity and grew rapidly.

Even though I tell every client that I can't promise a miracle nor even find anything that the client's doctor isn't aware of, I do have lots of success stories. A few years ago, I performed research for a woman in Canada with a ten-year history of debilitating ulcerative colitis. I found a brief summary (in English) from a Turkish medical journal about a treatment that was showing promise for exactly her type of ulcerative colitis. My client ordered the full article that, unlike the summary, was written in Turkish; she had it translated and talked her physician into trying it for her. At least for the time being, this new treatment has erased all her debilitating symptoms. Several clients have written to tell me that the information I found for them led to new and lifesaving treatments for their cancers.

I like to believe that Schine Online Services fits the category of something that improves the world just a little bit and uses business as the vehicle to do it. Though lots of people advised me to seek grants and similar types of support, my inclination was to improve the world through means of a lifestyle business. When approached from the right perspective, business can be an effective vehicle for making one's unique contribution to the world. That's what I tried to do with Schine Online Services.

Schedule Flexibility

Many people look to their own business as a way of gaining flexibility over their time. A parent who wants to spend more time with his or her children and needs a schedule that accommodates the children's schedule would fit this category. Although some organizations make allowances for working parents with childcare responsibilities, most do not, and those that do tend to do it in small incremental steps ("Yes, you can leave early on Tuesday as long as you come in early on Friday, but don't make a habit of it").

Schedule flexibility is certainly possible in the world of lifestyle businesses so long as the appropriate type of business is chosen at the outset. Retail businesses, at least the traditional brick-and-mortar kind, do not lend themselves to flexible scheduling, so they are not appropriate for those hoping to work when they please. Other businesses, primarily service and many Internet-related businesses, often do permit making one's own schedule.

ENTREPRENEUR PROFILE

Some People Insist on Schedule Flexibility

Quite often, various regions of the country experience shortages of nurses. Nurses, of course, are essential to hospitals, nursing homes, and other health facilities. They are needed 24 hours a day, and staffing shortages can mean that essential activities have to be curtailed.

Some years ago, the nursing shortage was particularly acute in New England. Certain medical facilities had to cut back some of their activities because of the shortage. Hospitals and nursing homes advertised heavily for nurses, offering signing bonuses and larger-than-usual pay differentials for some shifts. Yet the shortage persisted.

A client of mine, a person with no training in nursing or any other health-related profession, saw the shortage as an opportunity. She figured that the way to get more nurses was simply to offer unusually flexible work schedules, but this thinking didn't fit the mind-set of the organizations that needed the nurses. They were used to assigning nurses to fixed shifts and making the rules for modifications and exceptions to the shift schedules.

Jennifer set up a small office in a mall, reasoning that because women do most of the shopping and far more nurses are women than men, the mall would be a good place to find off-duty nurses. Her offer was simple yet radical. She merely told inquiring nurses, "Tell me what day(s) you want to work, what shift, and what area, and I'll place you." While the hospitals were still crying about shortages, nurses signed up with Jennifer in droves. Clearly, lots of nurses wanted to work but not if it meant accepting the restrictive scheduling rules of hospitals and nursing homes. Some wanted to spend time with their children, others wanted schedule flexibility, and so on. That's why Jennifer's offer was so attractive.

Jennifer made a lot of money. She contacted the people who were responsible for recruiting nurses and asked them to call her when they were temporarily short of staff, and she would be able to help. They called—desperately in many cases.

Jennifer would fill their needs and bill them approximately twice as much for a shift as she was paying the nurse she sent. Hospitals had little choice but to pay her rate.

Jennifer was a smart businesswoman in several ways. But the biggest key to her entrepreneurial success was noticing and acting on a desire that at least some nurses had to fit work into their lifestyle rather than the other way around.

Making Your Hobby Your Business

Still other lifestyle entrepreneurs look at work as a means primarily of paying their bills and at pursuits, such as travel or hobbies, as their reason for being. The ideal job is one that can be performed around recreational needs and not the more traditional reverse.

A number of people in this group aspire to make their hobby their business (see the entrepreneur profile in Chapter 5: Apartments in Europe). This, too, is a real possibility for the lifestyle entrepreneur. A current client of mine, who is an avid knitter, started a business 20 years ago from her apartment selling knitting supplies by mail order. Though knitting, and not business, remains her passion, she had sales of nearly $4 million last year.

A warning: Once your hobby becomes your business and livelihood, it may by nature lose the allure it had as a hobby. Gardening during leisure time in the springtime is not the same as selling seeds through the mail, nor is it the same as selling produce at a farmers market. Be sure the aspects that make your hobby fun remain fun once it becomes a business. If it does, then it's is a viable option.

Creative Expression

Andy Warhol once said, "Making money is art and working is art, and good business is the best art of all," (*The Philosophy of Andy Warhol,* Harcourt, 1975).

When I had just completed my MBA, I moved to Providence, Rhode Island. Something that struck me about the city was the number of businesses started by graduates and professors from the Rhode Island School of Design (RISD), which is located in Providence. In fact, I learned that RISD grads are far more likely to start their own business than are new MBAs.

Although at the time this surprised me, I now understand it. Artists are by their nature creative people. That creativity can be expressed through the traditional arts like painting, sculpture, dance, or film, but it doesn't stop there for those who think creatively. It can also be expressed through conceiving, designing, and building one's own company.

Business students, on the other hand, tend to be more traditional in their view of the world; analysis, team building, and ladder climbing are the values taught in business school. Creativity and risk taking are not as highly valued. Taking risks that can't easily be calculated and betting on one's own creativity over the tried and true is hardly encouraged in most business school programs.

Art schools encourage different thinking. Students attend an art school like RISD largely because they thrive on creativity rather than on empirical analysis and incremental ladder climbing. Art professors, unlike business professors, encourage—in fact demand—creativity and self-expression. It's little wonder that many of the kids who have a long history of creative expression and are encouraged to continue expressing their own voice choose small business as the vehicle for self-expression. Rather than learn the culture and rules of standard professions and occupations, artists are more comfortable creating their own rules and their own professions and businesses.

A good example of this artist-to-business phenomenon is that of Al Forno Restaurant which was started in 1978 by a married couple—he a former RISD sculptor professor and she a photography major. At the outset, George and Johanne decided that their restaurant would not copy food preparation styles of any other restaurant. As "card-carrying" artists, they invented their own style of cooking and built their restaurant around such signature dishes as wood-grilled pizza and made-to-order desserts. To say their restaurant worked out well is an understatement; Al Forno is one of the country's most successful restaurants in business terms and especially in terms of creative cooking. It regularly wins top cooking awards and is widely considered one of the ten best restaurants in the country for innovative cooking. George and Johanne are still there doing some of the cooking and regularly creating new dishes.

What the various lifestyle entrepreneurs have in common is a desire to get something more out of business, indeed out of life, than financial rewards. This is not to say that lifestyle entrepreneurs don't expect or want to make money from their businesses. It *is* to say that money is only one of the returns they want to see from their efforts.

Lifestyle entrepreneurs tend to aim for a *well-considered life.* They want to decide what is important to them and how they spend their time. They don't want to blindly accept the values of a larger and more established group such as a corporation, which means they want to set their own goals, values, and priorities. A relatively free society like ours offers this opportunity; if you can conceive it and do it, go ahead. But nothing in our laws or culture forces us to take advantage of our freedoms nor even makes it easy for us to do so. It is far easier to choose from the several templated sets of values and definitions of success offered by family, school, company, and other organizational entities. If you're one of those who can't find a set of values that fit, or you just aren't interested in looking, small business or self-employment may offer the vehicle to exercise your own custom-made values and priorities.

Although a small business can be a ticket to freedom, success does demand adherence to certain realities and principles. The content and direction of a business is largely controlled by the entrepreneur who conceives and runs it as long as it is earning income and following the basic ground rules and structures set by various government authorities.

Perceptions and Reactions of Others

When I was finishing business school, a group of soon-to-be MBAs were talking about our postgraduation plans. One student had just landed a job with NCR and another with Proctor & Gamble; and several others proudly shared news of their future employer. When someone asked me what I'd be doing, I responded that I'd be starting a business. I hoped someone would be curious enough to ask for more details, but no one did. Instead, a brief silence fell at the table, soon broken by a classmate saying, "So you haven't been able to find a job huh?" Some in the group found this mildly humorous, and I suspect also believed it to be the truth.

A lot of years have passed since I finished business school, and entrepreneurship has gained a good deal of respectability since then. Starting one's own company has gained acceptance, perhaps even prestige. I'll bet a group of new MBAs talking about their plans today would view a colleague who intends to start a company instead of working for an existing one with a lot less skepticism and a lot more positive interest. I doubt the phrase "I'm starting a company" would be considered tantamount to "I haven't found a job yet."

Entrepreneurship may have come of age, but there is a wide range of perceptions your friends, colleagues, and coworkers will exhibit and reactions you can expect. Some will be positive, some negative. Many will be based partly on a misunderstanding of what small business is about. Most will say more about the person who is responding to your plans than they will about your plans or yourself.

Perceptions of coworkers and colleagues. Some people, including a few coworkers, will envy you. They mostly envy the chutzpa you demonstrate by going off on your own and the perceived freedom that comes with business ownership. People reacting with envy may be thinking, "Wow, she will have her own business and all sorts of freedom and prestige while I'll be stuck here for who knows how long." Of course, they may gloss over the risks and other hardships you'll be taking to achieve your business goals.

At the other end of the reaction spectrum, some will pity you. Remember, the response will have more to do with others' own perceptions, personalities, and fears than with your plans. Again, many who react this way are coworkers and colleagues, who'll talk about the security and benefits you'll be giving up. You may hear scare stories about friends who tried starting their own business with disastrous results. The "pitiers" will doubtless be tactful and polite, but they will be thinking, "How can he be so stupid? Doesn't he understand that he has a great deal here? Why would he give it up?"

Other people, perhaps the majority, will be clueless about how to react; they won't comprehend the framework of self-employment. In reality, only a small percentage of the population ever even considers working for themselves. Most people think of work as something you do for someone else, probably and preferably a big organization that gives you a paycheck each week and decides how big that paycheck will be. The idea of having the freedom and control to assume the employer's role, even to employ only one's self, is simply beyond the comprehension of most employees.

The clueless people may ask about rules and regulations because their frame of reference insists that some authority must approve a plan so bold as this. Don't you have to get a license or something from some government authority? Somehow, all that stuff they learned in high school about our free economy can't possibly apply on the day-to-day work level. But it does.

Lots of people from the various groups I've described will find problems and pitfalls with your plans. You'll get such well-meaning questions as these: "How will you find customers? Where will you get the money to start? Isn't it risky? What if this happens or that happens? These questions are legitimate, but you have lessened your risks if you are properly prepared. Even though the risk itself may not thrill you, if you've read this far, you consider the risk worth taking to gain the independence of lifestyle that you seek.

Don't be discouraged by the reactions of coworkers and colleagues. Again, these reactions have more to do with the people doing the reacting than with you or your plans. Keep in mind that you are getting a skewed sample of reactions from coworkers and colleagues. These are people who work for an employer. Were they of an entrepreneurial mind-set, they would be either in their own business or at least preparing to be, as you are.

Other self-employed and small business people. If you are able to talk to people who are self-employed or involved in small business, by all means do so. If you can talk to self-employed people who are in your field, all the better. You'll get an entirely different reaction and, I dare say, a much more useful one. You will get pointed and pragmatic questions such as these: Have you planned your sales approach? Do you have a list of prospects? These people won't spend a lot of time questioning the concept of entrepreneurship but will concentrate on the practical details, including important ones you may have overlooked. They won't concentrate on the what-if disaster scenarios nor will they have overly romantic notions of small business that your employed friends may have. They know what it's all about because they live it.

These people have been through business start-up and have lots of relevant experience to draw on. Whether they tell you what you want to hear or not, their advice comes more from their business experience than from misinformation and supposition. The only caveat is that you may not hear exactly what you want to hear, and they may find problems and shortcomings that you overlooked. It's better for you to learn about these problems now from experienced entrepreneurs than later from the unforgiving marketplace.

Not a real business. Despite the fact that entrepreneurship is more respectable now than it was just a few years ago, some people still don't consider a small business a *real* business. I'm regularly amused by people, including businesspeople, who scoff at very small companies as somehow illegitimate. Now I could understand, though not approve of, the scoffing at fledgling businesses that are not yet earning an income for their owner. But size of income doesn't seem to matter to the scoffers. A lot of people look down on self-employed people—even those who are making a good deal of money, have a stable client base, and have lifestyle freedom. Somehow, a large business is a real business, even if its owner is not breaking even. And somehow a big company job is better, even if the income is smaller than that of a self-employed person, the hours are longer, and freedom is nonexistent. If the affiliation and title granted by a big company are worth more than the lifestyle freedom of self-employment, then the lifestyle business route is simply not for you.

It's always struck me as strange that so many people (including businesspeople who should know better) consider the top line (gross sales) to be more important than the bottom line (earnings). Which is better: a lifestyle business grossing $60,000 whose owner earns $50,000 or a $1 million business whose owner isn't breaking even? To me, the lifestyle business is the better one by far—especially if the lifestyle entrepreneur may have almost no overhead to tie him down and probably loves his job. Others, many others, would choose the $1 million business, even when faced with this logic; at $1 million, after all, for them it can at least be considered a *real* business.

To this point, I've talked a lot about the concept of lifestyle entrepreneurship and pointed out the differences between the lifestyle entrepreneur and the more traditional entrepreneur.

I've also discussed the reasons so many people decide that self-employment can be their ticket to the lifestyle they desire, and I've shared some examples of successful lifestyle entrepreneurs.

But business requires more than conceptual discussion—it requires doing. Plans need to be made and concrete steps taken. The rest of this book focuses on the doing. It's now time to detail the steps that have to be taken to get your business started and meet the challenges of becoming a successful lifestyle entrepreneur.

CHAPTER

2

What Is a Business? (Basic Elements)

I've argued that lifestyle businesses, in many ways, are very different from traditional businesses. At a basic level, though, every business, whether it's Microsoft, the local dry cleaner, or a one-person graphic arts company, faces a few of the same core issues and tasks in order to survive. These include income, legal structure, planning and overall management, financial management, and marketing. The following sections discuss each of these in turn.

Income

To survive, a business must take in at least enough money to meet its expenses. Some new businesses with ample financing can and do initially operate at a loss for several months, even years. Eventually, though, even the best-financed ventures can't survive as businesses if they can't meet their expenses. Of course, this is the minimum criterion. Few business owners are satisfied to merely take in enough to meet their expenses—they want and expect to earn a profit. For purposes of this book, meeting and exceeding expenses pretty much constitute the foremost criteria for defining a business.

Legal Structure

A business must be structured as a legal entity. Contrary to what many fledgling entrepreneurs think, the business does not have to be a corporation; in fact, many of the businesses that readers of this book will start don't have to be corporations, at least not in their beginning. However, a business without a purposefully chosen legal structure will by default be a *sole proprietorship.* Significant legal (and financial and tax) ramifications are based on a business's legal structure, whether purposefully chosen by you or chosen for you by default. (For more information on legal structure, See Chapter 7.)

Planning and Overall Management

I once read that if you don't train your dog, your dog will train itself. We've all met dogs who follow their own rules rather than those set by their owners; dogs well trained by their owners, however, make far better pets than self-trained, laissez-faire dogs.

Businesses that are not adequately planned and managed by their owners, like dogs, can and do get into a great deal of trouble, if they survive at all. Yes, there are businesses that seemingly run without direction by their owners or managers; but few of these autopilot companies survive, and fewer still grow and thrive. Running a business, no matter how small, requires vigilance over many aspects, ranging from servicing customers to purchasing supplies to pricing and promotion. Bad management is far and away the leading cause of business failures.

Financial Management

I was once consulting for a photography business owned by three people. After taking a look at their bank statement, their bills due (accounts payable), and the bills due them (accounts receivables), I called the owners into an emergency meeting. I explained that they were about to have a cash flow problem so serious that meeting their bills as soon as next month could be a problem. They looked at me suspiciously and asked, "Well, how do you know this?" I explained that I had looked over their finances and did some simple calculations. Unconvinced, they asked, "Has the bank bounced any checks?" It hadn't (yet). "Well, then how can we have a cash flow problem?"

It seems almost too obvious to mention, but a business has to manage its financial affairs to stay in business. A business having difficulties paying its bills will have difficulty obtaining products and services it needs to function and is obviously on tenuous grounds. Keeping an eye on finances and planning in advance for bills due are essential for maintaining good standing and good credit. Waiting until the bank bounces checks is hardly a good planning strategy. For most businesses, financial management involves a bit more than merely paying bills. Issues like managing credit prudently, getting paid on time, and general management of money are discussed in detail in Chapter 9 (as usual from the point of view of the lifestyle entrepreneur).

Taxes

As complex as our tax system may be for people whose primary income comes from an employer, it is even more complex for businesses, even very small businesses. Fortunately, few small business people have to master all the complexities of the federal and state tax codes, but they do need to be aware of issues that affect them directly. Simple legal techniques can easily make differences of hundreds, even thousands, of dollars in your pocket.

Moreover, business owners are responsible for complying with tax payments, tax reporting, and even tax collection from others (sales tax) in some cases. On the other side of the coin, a number of benefits may be available to you as a small business owner, such as tax credits and deductions, that weren't previously available to you as an employee. For example, under current tax law for small businesses, it is possible (and legal) through tax planning for the government, in essence, to pay up to one-half the cost of your new computer, office furniture, or other equipment you need to run your company. However, the seemingly insignificant difference of buying that furniture on December 31 versus on January 1 can mean the difference between a tax benefit worth a couple of thousand dollars and no benefit at all. Be sure to talk to your accountant regarding tax and reporting issues and about strategies for minimizing the tax burden on your company and yourself.

Marketing

If a man can write a better book,
preach a better sermon, or make a better mousetrap,
. . . his neighbor will make a beaten path to his door.

—RALPH WALDO EMERSON

Perhaps in the 1800s, when Mr. Emerson said this, it was true; but in the 21st century, it is decidedly a recipe for small business disaster. Every company must market its product or service.

Many people equate marketing with advertising or promotion. In reality, advertising and promotion are only a few of the elements of marketing. Others are distribution (getting the product or service to the customer), price, and the product itself. Not every company needs media advertising, and some don't need to advertise at all in the traditional sense. But every company does need to consider the ways in which its prospective customers will learn about its products and services, how it will get the services to its customers, and the prices it will charge for those products and services. There is a huge range of methods that companies employ to market their offerings, and the most obvious—advertising—is only the tip of the iceberg. (Marketing is discussed in more detail in Chapter 5.)

It's a Great Idea, but Is It a Business?

Someone once said of William Paley, the founder of CBS, that "he knew what was good and he knew what would sell, and he never confused the two. The point is that people won't necessarily pay for what may be good or even what they need, no matter how overwhelming the proof of goodness or need. It is essential to know, or to quickly determine, what people will pay for when you're trying to sell something to them. (Methods of determining whether your product or service is marketable are presented in Chapter 4.)

One of the biggest difficulties I see in those who fit my profile as lifestyle entrepreneurs is that they don't, or won't, understand the difference between what should be and what is. Traditional entrepreneurs have no such problem; what's good is what people will buy at a price that yields a nice profit. Just because you think something is a good idea and are convinced—and can prove—that people need it doesn't necessarily mean it's a good business idea. In a free marketplace, people can accept or reject just about any product or service they want to for just about any reason, whether that reason makes sense or not. Undoubtedly, many excellent products fail and many bad ones succeed.

The question to be answered, by actual testing if possible (see Chapter 4), is *will* they buy it, *not should* they buy it. Even if they will buy it, the next question is will they buy it at a price at which you can make some money. Clearly, you can't stay in business too long if you're buying something for $10 and reselling it for $9. But even if you're buying it for $10 and selling it for $20, it's not a viable business if it costs you an average of $11 in marketing expense to find and acquire each customer who will buy it for that price.

For example, direct mail businesses typically resell products for at least double the amount for which they buy them. This may seem an easy way to make lots of money, but most direct mail firms' catalogs and brochures end up in wastebaskets with no accompanying orders. As a rule of thumb (though it varies a great deal from industry to industry and company to company), a response rate of 2 percent from a direct mailing is considered pretty good. If a catalog costs $1.00 to produce and $0.50 to mail, and 98 of 100 are discarded, the company doing the mailing has in essence paid $150 to acquire 2 customers. If the company doubles the price it pays for each product, those 2 customers have to order $300 worth of stuff for the company to break even, and that doesn't include overhead costs like telephones, office space, warehousing, and so on. This example is oversimplified to make the basic point that you have to evaluate a product's or service's money-making potential in the world as it is, not as it perhaps should be.

Keep It Simple

An aspiring businessman once came to me for advice about a planned new business venture that involved importing products into the United States via American Indian reservations, thereby giving the products a duty advantage. He explained the concept but glossed over the fact that in addition to the usual start-up challenges, the venture would also require a waiver from Congress. Now if AT&T or General Motors wants to pursue a new line of business that requires congressional approval, that approval may not be an insurmountable obstacle. For a lone entrepreneur, however, a business requiring congressional approval is probably too complex or at least too costly and time consuming to pursue.

Many small businesses fail to get off the ground because they are also too complex or too ambitious. Entrepreneurs (in this instance I make no distinction between traditional and lifestyle entrepreneurs) tend to brush aside obstacles that can impede a fledgling business. You should be able to see a clear path from where you are to where you can sell your product or service and make money. The fewer obstacles and blind spots in that path, the better. Or as someone once said (though I confess, I don't know who), "If it doesn't work on the back of an envelope, it ain't gonna work."

Two questions you should ask yourself:

1. *Who are your target customers?* If you can't identify the group or groups that will consider buying your product, you have a major problem with the concept. You should understand the people who make up your target market—their needs, buying habits, perceptions, and the like. At the very least, be sure that they exist and that you know who they are.

2. *How can you reach your customers?* You need a way (preferably several ways) to reach your prospective customers with your message. You don't have to reach every single possible prospect, but you do have to reach enough of them to give yourself a fair chance of making enough sales to make money. What's more, you have to be able to reach your prospects cheaply enough to pay your marketing costs out of sales and still have money left over to pay your expenses (and I hope more than that).

Suppose you're a teacher with a great method to help children who are performing poorly in geometry, and you want to offer your services privately. You need a way to find parents of students with that problem—and who also perceive it as a problem in need of a solution. There is probably no publication dedicated to poor math students (or their parents), and schools won't sell lists of all students who scored below a C in geometry class.

Sure, you can pay for broad advertising on radio or TV, reasoning that some percentage of those reached will need your services. But the name of the game in small business is *niche marketing*. Paying for broad-based advertising for a niche service like this one is unlikely to be economical. Because of the tremendous reach of broadcast TV, rates are set for those selling products with mass appeal. Lots of people buy beer and deodorants, so the cost of mass advertising those products is justified. Few people (at least relative to mass market products) buy remedial geometry services, no matter how good those services may be. (Marketing is covered in detail in Chapter 5.)

It's a Great Idea, but Will It Fit Your Lifestyle?

Lifestyle entrepreneurs have more to consider than if it will work. As such an entrepreneur, you also must consider if it will fit your chosen lifestyle.

A pillar of traditional business rationale is to earn a return on your investment. It's hard to argue against this principle, but it does need modification for lifestyle entrepreneurs because it doesn't include personal preferences and nonmonetary goals. An example is seen in hiring employees. Traditional wisdom would argue that if an employee would cost $500 per week and the income derived from that employee would be a stable $600 per week, the hiring should be done; end of story. Does this logic work, however, if the owner of the business just doesn't want employees because he perceives them as a headache? Does avoiding that headache have a dollar value? Once again, though, traditional wisdom doesn't take into account the needs of the kind of entrepreneur this book is designed to help.

Some years ago, wearing my business broker hat, I helped the owner of a machine shop sell his business. The business was doing reasonably well, but the owner had grown tired and frustrated with it. A few months after the sale, he called me to say he wanted to buy a new business (this isn't unusual; after small business owners sell out, they often want to get back into business a few months later). When I asked what kind of business he was looking to buy, his response: "My ideal business is one that I can run with no employees." Clearly, what turned him off to the business he sold was managing and generally dealing with employees. Although this kind of "ideal business scenario" makes little sense in the traditional business world, it makes plenty of sense—and in fact is not unusual—in the lifestyle business world.

Many lifestyle entrepreneurs go into their own business largely because they don't want to rely on others or be responsible for others. With the advent of office technology and the Internet, running a business without employees is quite doable today, as long as you choose the right business and set it up the right way. It may work well for most professional services and certain Internet ventures, for example, but it would seldom work well for a manufacturing venture or a brick-and-mortar retail store.

Does It Involve Significant Up-Front Investment?

There's nothing wrong with up-front investment in equipment, research, development, and the like so long as you do it with your eyes open and it can ultimately pay for itself. Keep in mind that the bigger the investment, the more you are likely to be tied to the business. If your reason for going into business is so you can have the freedom to travel several times a year on a whim, a business with significant up-front investment might prove more of a burden than you want to take on. If you borrow $50,000 to buy equipment, the lender, be it a bank or a relative, doesn't want to hear "Oh, I won't be paying the June or July payment because I'll be traveling in Asia then." The lender expects you to be working that equipment to keep those monthly payments coming in.

Does It Require Ploughing Back Earnings into the Business?

Several kinds of businesses are profitable on the surface but require a lot of their profits to be invested back into the business. Companies that rely heavily on advanced technology fit this profile. Prepress companies (color separators), for example, prepare color drawings and photos for printing by color printers. The technology to do this is expensive and, moreover, is constantly improving. To remain competitive means to remain on the cutting edge of the technology. And to remain on the cutting edge of technology means constantly reinvesting profits to buy newer and better prepress equipment.

Again, this kind of situation may be appropriate for the traditional entrepreneur focused on the goal of growing a business but less appropriate for the lifestyle entrepreneur looking for a flexible lifestyle not dominated by his or her business.

The Magic Post Office Box Principle

Are there major obstacles at the outset? Every new venture faces obstacles when getting started. Not only do you need financing, marketing, and plans for achieving sales and profitability, but you have competition to deal with. However, some ventures face fewer and less daunting obstacles than do others. Your chance of success is greatest where you can see a straight line from inception to sales and profits with as few large obstacles in the way as possible. Keep it simple.

Years ago, when I attended a conference on small business and entrepreneurship, a Harvard professor gave a speech in which he argued that "the perfect small business is a post office box to which people send money." No, he hadn't lost his sense of the real world. His point was that small business owners tend to add complexities to their business that they assume are essential but that don't really need to be there.

Start with the theoretical magic post office box as an ideal and then add overhead and complexities as required and justified, not the other way around. If your gross sales and hours worked would be the same whether you worked alone at home or in a rented office with an assistant, why not do it the cheaper way? Don't assume that a business needs an office, a secretary, a computer system, or expensive furniture to do well. If any or all of those things are needed from a business perspective, by all means get them. The magic post office box earning $50,000 per year is better than the business based in a glitzy office tower with fancy furniture and a new computer system but earns only $30,000 per year.

CHAPTER

3

On Becoming a Lifestyle Entrepreneur

I'll spare the usual warnings about how hard you'll have to work to get started, the sacrifices you'll have to make, and the personality profile tests designed to see *if you've got what it takes* to be on your own. Many books offer comprehensive warnings about these kinds of lifestyle sacrifices and psychological characteristics that are needed to fit the entrepreneurial stereotype. As should be obvious by now, my point of view is a bit different—I assume not everyone who wants to have his or her own business wants to or needs to fit the stereotype.

Having said that, there are nonetheless certain psychological characteristics and issues to consider that are important to entering and thriving in the entrepreneurial life. If you have these traits innately and have considered these issues, you're at an advantage. If you don't have the traits, you can develop them, at least to a degree sufficient to run a lifestyle business.

Why Do You Want to Be a Lifestyle Entrepreneur?

First and foremost, you should be crystal clear why you want to be a lifestyle entrepreneur. I can pretty much guarantee there will be risks, sacrifices, and other hardships along the way. So before signing on, it would be helpful to know why you're putting yourself through the challenges that you will face.

Beyond defining the *why,* you also need to carefully consider how your business will help you meet your lifestyle objectives. If your reason for wanting to start a business is to have more time to spend with your kids, and your business concept involves storefront retail, your method is probably not in line with your objective. There is nothing wrong with running a retail shop for someone whose main goal is to meet lots of people who are interested in the kinds of goods that shop is selling. However, retail shops demand lots of fixed work hours and, more likely than not, lots of late afternoon, weekend, and even holiday hours—hardly the best structure for someone looking to spend time with kids on a school schedule.

On the other hand, if time flexibility is your main goal, a Web-based retail business may work quite well for you. Although your online store can be open 24 hours a day, you can fill your orders, plan your marketing, and pay your bills any time you wish. Of course, if your goal is to get out of the house and meet people, an online business just won't cut it.

A good exercise would be to list your goals concisely in order of their importance to you. Are you considering starting your business to practice a field you love? Or is your goal to contribute to the world with business as your vehicle, or is it to enable you to pursue your passion for travel? Is increasing your income a top priority? Perhaps your most important goal is setting up a business that can involve your children on a day-to-day basis.

The rest of the exercise is to list the ways in which your business concept will help you reach your goals and then list the impediments you may face along the way. If you're going into business because you want to practice the field you love on your own terms, consider how much time you will spend running the business rather than practicing the field that your business is supposed to enable? If your goal is to travel for months at a time, can you realistically structure your business to permit that kind of time flexibility? A business that caters to, say winter tourists in a ski area, may well permit such escapades in the summer months, whereas one with clients expecting services year round does not.

Despite my being a dedicated advocate of lifestyle entrepreneurship, I also advocate proceeding with caution. There is no point in going through the effort of setting up a lifestyle business if it won't help you toward your lifestyle goals. So before proceeding any further, please honestly assess how your business and its structure will and won't help you toward your lifestyle goals.

The Reality of Risk

By its nature, any new business involves risk, so anyone planning to go into business must be prepared to accept a certain degree of risk. However, this doesn't mean a would-be lifestyle entrepreneur has to be a high-risk taker or gambler; in fact, quite the opposite. Although the stereotypical (and mythical) entrepreneur is a big risk taker, the reality is very different. Most entrepreneurs are comfortable with modest risk but quite uncomfortable with big risks. Further, most entrepreneurs greatly prefer risks in which they can influence, if not fully control, the outcome.

Joe Mancuso, a professor and author of books about small business, has studied the issue of entrepreneurs and risk, and had this to say:

> Entrepreneurs seem to thrive on the 3 to 1 shot—a gamble they judge to be exciting but realistic.
>
> Although they are unwilling to gamble on long shots, they are more willing to take a chance if their individual skills can affect the probability of success. (*How to Start, Finance, and Manage Your Own Small Business,* Prentice Hall, 1984, p. 7.)

A good friend of mine is a wealthy businessperson who has owned 15 different businesses over the years. He is ready, willing, and able to invest in new small business opportunities and does in fact make one or two investments a year, risking several hundred thousand dollars of his own money. However, he very seldom invests in the stock market. Money he has that is not invested in small, privately owned business ventures is invested very conservatively in corporate and government bonds. For someone who is not shy about investing in high-risk small companies, his investment strategy vis-à-vis to public companies seems uncharacteristically conservative.

When I asked him about this, his reply came quickly: "Sure, I can buy shares of IBM or Microsoft or any other publicly traded company. But even if I invested all my money in any one of these companies, I would not have control nor even significant influence over what happens to that investment. When I invest in a small company, I'm taking a much bigger risk to be sure, but I have a good measure of control over how that investment turns out." That illustrates the philosophy regarding risk held by many entrepreneurs: risk is acceptable when I have some control over the outcome.

So, in essence, you need confidence in your ability to do what you set out to do, because you'll have ultimate control and ultimate decision-making authority. You won't be able to blame an incompetent boss or colleague or coworker or anyone else. Further, customers and clients will come with their own personal needs and idiosyncrasies. They won't comply with your needs and won't even necessarily be reasonable, at least from your perspective. Nevertheless, you'll have to deal with them as they are and take responsibility for the outcome of your customer relations efforts.

Failure Is a Possibility

By definition, risk means the outcome may or may not go the way you hope it will. A corollary to accepting risk is accepting the possibility, and sometimes the reality, of failure. In small business as in life, things don't always work out as planned and hoped. I can't recall any successful entrepreneurs I know who haven't had at least a few business failures along the way. But they don't dwell on the failures. Rather, they look at them as bumps in the road and unfortunate exceptions—and, in some cases, valuable learning opportunities.

Some people, in fact, argue that a true entrepreneur is someone not afraid to fail. The person who tries one business venture, sees it fail, and then never tries again is hardly an entrepreneur. The person who tries a venture, sees it fail, gets up, brushes himself off, and asks, "How can I learn from this for next time?" is the entrepreneur I'd bet on.

There will be disappointments. They may or may not be as big as the failure of an entire venture, but you'll have ideas that don't pan out, sales that are lost, advertising efforts that don't yield results, and more. This is the definition of risk: some things work, some don't. Capitalize on the winners and learn from the failures.

Learn to Be Analytical and Objective

Much of the coursework in an MBA program involves learning the various facets of modern business. Like other MBA students, I studied marketing, accounting, finance, and general management. By far the most important principle I learned, however, was not the focus of any particular course. That principle was the need to objectively think through and analyze business problems and opportunities. There is little room in business school or in business for wishful thinking or supposition. There is room for judgment, even for gut feeling, but they need to be objectively analyzed with full consideration of the known facts and research. More important, there must be an overall business objective—a framework for proceeding according to a clear and stated direction. That framework can be to become a public company within five years; in the world of lifestyle entrepreneurship, it can be to limit your work to 20 hours per week so you can write, or ski, or spend more time with your family. Obviously, a company with the former goal would make different decisions along the way than a company with the latter goal. The point is that the business direction would be set based on the chosen objectives, and decisions along the way could be evaluated based on those objectives.

Problems and opportunities need to be evaluated based on their challenges and merits and their impact on the overall objectives and purpose of the business. Though few business professors would approve of, or even understand, the objectives of a lifestyle business, such objectives are no less legitimate than more traditional business objectives like going public or dominating a niche. Though the ends may differ, lifestyle entrepreneurs must apply the same objective analysis to their businesses that other business managers do.

It is often helpful to clearly define a problem or opportunity and list three or four different options for dealing with that problem or opportunity. In this analytic way, the most appropriate option for a given situation can be chosen, based on well thought-out criteria. For example, suppose you're a self-employed computer programmer accustomed to short-term projects that pay \$3,000 to \$5,000. Then suppose you are asked by a company to prepare a proposal for a contract that would involve on-site work at seven different locations in the United States and Europe. The job has to be completed in three months; it involves programming in a language that you don't know. The job would therefore require at least one other programmer who knows that language. The entire contract would be in the \$30,000 to \$50,000 range. You define your four options as follows:

1. Pass on the job entirely.
2. Contact a larger programming company that you've worked with in the past and make a deal to try to get the

job for them with a commission for yourself as well as some of the work.

3. Do the proposal as requested and be ready to hire the requisite programmer at a moment's notice; also be ready to gear up for a job ten times the size of your normal jobs.

4. Try to persuade the company to work with you on the parts you can readily handle and offer to assist them in (but not take responsibility for) finding another programmer for the parts you can't handle.

Any one of these options is viable. However, if you were committed to being a lifestyle entrepreneur with the business objective of limiting your work-time commitments, the third option is probably not your best one. On the other hand, if your aspiration is to grow rapidly, the opportunity offered by option 3 could be seen as your potential big break, so only the third option would make sense.

Sometimes the outcome of an objective analysis of your business needs runs counter to the objectives of your profession. Following business school, I reentered the video production business. By applying the analytical tools of business that I had learned, a problem became apparent. Sometimes, the best decision from a business perspective is not the best decision from a video production perspective. It is invariably more economical to get a job done in the least amount of time possible, because every additional day taken to complete a job increases expenses and lowers the profit margin. However, video production is partly an art, and time constraints are therefore not well tolerated. Translation: sometimes we had to make choices between an adequate video that was profitable or an artistically superb video that was less profitable.

Different people may have made different decisions in a circumstance like this. There may be no universal right or wrong, but in certain situations an objective analysis will yield a better answer from a business perspective. To the extent that it's reasonable, business decisions should be based on an objective analysis of a situation and the available data as well as in keeping with your overall objectives.

Prioritizing and Organizing

Over the years I've had the opportunity to observe hundreds of businesses as a consultant and as a business broker. In both roles I'm privy to the inner workings of the businesses I'm looking at—their marketing, finances, overall management, and overall success. One of my pet observations is that many very successful businesspeople attribute their success to their abilities—some going as far as saying their genius—in marketing, finance, or human relations. However, I find that their genius is seldom in the areas where they believe it to be but rather is in their ability to organize and prioritize.

On the surface, these businesspeople may not appear to be superorganized. Their desks are typically a mess of papers with no defined place for each paper and folder. But they also have detailed checklists of things to do in order of priority and detailed schedules for what they (and others) will be doing and when. They tend to have folders or notebooks that each details various facets of their business, such as folders for active customers, inactive customers, competitors, investor prospects, and promotional materials.

Most of the successful business owners I've observed have the ability to prioritize tasks, opportunities, and problems and then methodically organize a strategy for dealing with those tasks. They can keep their eye on the overall objective without getting sidetracked by daily brush fires; a letter from the IRS won't mean they stop everything to fret over the letter. They can compartmentalize tasks and projects and deal with each when it is most appropriate to do so.

I'm not sure if the key is just knowing what's important or declaring something important and sticking with that declaration. But I do know that constant changing of priorities is a recipe for trouble. Those businesspeople I see who get into trouble tend to change their priorities regularly, not have any priorities to begin with, or have priorities but no organized strategy for keeping to those priorities without getting sidetracked.

A newly self-employed medical billing collection consultant may decide that one effective strategy is to sponsor seminars on effective collection techniques for administrators of physicians' offices. Another possibility is to actually set up a collection service for medical offices. Either strategy may work if pursued, but making both work concurrently would be exceedingly difficult. Ideally, an objective analysis might point clearly to one or the other as being the better of the two. In the real world, though, there are often shades of gray, so we could see pros and cons for either strategy. Choosing one and running with it offers a reasonable chance for success. Choosing one, running with it for a while, changing to the other, and changing back and forth is a recipe for frustration and failure.

I once had a client who wanted to go into the software design business—or into software consulting and systems consulting. She couldn't decide, so, you guessed it, she did both and therefore did neither very well. Her marketing was disjointed as was her entire organization. Her resources were limited, and she had difficulty deciding how to allocate those limited resources of time, money, and effort. Unfortunately, the business failed. Had she pursued one or the other, would the business have succeeded? It's hard to know, and it's hard to know which of the two possible directions would have been the better choice. I would argue, however, that her chances would have been a lot better had she based her decision on the best (albeit imperfect) information available and her lifestyle needs, prioritized her tasks, and set out to tackle those tasks without changing priorities at every challenging obstacle.

This isn't to advise against flexibility. In fact, flexibility is essential because no plan or strategy works in real life exactly as it does on paper. There is a difference, though, between being flexible enough to make appropriate adjustments to a strategy and the wholesale discarding of one strategy in favor of another or no strategy at all.

Much of this book talks about the various aspects of up-front planning and organizing for a business, particularly a lifestyle business. Planning such aspects as marketing, financing, and technology are covered, but the overall lesson I learned in business school is the overall lesson you should learn too. It is essential to make plans and run your business based on objective analysis guided by an overall strategy. Doing this defines the business itself and the reasons for that business to exist. The marketing, financial, and technical aspects are the tools for building that business and keeping it sound.

Your Value and Your Hourly Rate

To many people, including most who work for an employer, compensation is based on time worked; you may get paid so much per hour, per week, or per year. Regardless of the period on which your pay is based, there is a tangible ratio between time worked and dollars received. And many new lifestyle entrepreneurs carry this thinking over into their own business.

"I'm worth $50 per hour so that's what I'll charge (or $500 per day, or $2,000 per week, etc.)." With a few exceptions, customers and clients ultimately think in terms of value of benefits received, not amount paid per hour. If you're hiring someone to paint your house, you probably expect a quotation for the job, not a per-day charge. Certainly, if you're buying a car, a house, or just about any other product, you don't want to hear that the price depends on how long it takes to assemble the product.

In some instances—tutoring or most types of psychotherapy, for example—charging by the hour may be the only way to go. Whenever practical, though, it's better to charge by the job than by the hour. In all likelihood, you'll earn more in the long run if you charge this way, but, regardless, you'll have smoother relations with your customers or clients if they are paying for a completed job without worrying how long it may take you.

Don't think in these terms: "This is how much I'm worth." Think instead in terms of getting the maximum revenue possible by balancing the sales you'll achieve against the time, effort, and expense needed to consummate those sales and deliver the product or service. In reality, the marketplace, not you, determines what your time (actually your product or service) is worth. Confusing your concept of your worth with the marketplace value of the benefits of your product or service is a recipe for trouble.

Another problem with charging by the hour is the misunderstanding common to people who aren't in their own business that charging $80 an hour doesn't mean you make $80 an hour for 40 hours a week. It is not uncommon for someone to hear a quoted fee of $80 per hour, for example, and start calculating your earnings without considering your office, marketing, other expenses, and the fact that you probably don't get paid for all the hours you work. If that person earns perhaps $20 per hour at a salaried job, he or she may resent the perception that you make four times as much (of course, brushing aside that you have expenses, take significant financial risks, etc.). It's best to prevent these kinds of comparisons by quoting and charging based on the completed job, whenever possible. The amount of time it takes to do the job is your business. The customer's concern is that you deliver the product or service you agreed to deliver.

Charging by the hour from a marketing perspective is discussed in Chapter 5.

Being the Best versus Being Perceived the Best

I introduced this book by telling the story of my sister, the karate teacher, but I didn't talk about the difficulties she had in getting started. Bobbie had the idea of teaching karate to women about two years before she actually set up on her own to do it. She talked a few colleges and community centers into letting her teach a few classes, partly to test the concept. The courses were well received and well attended, but she was still troubled and confessed to me that she knew many women were better than she was at karate. Further, at the time she was a mere brown belt, whereas most of the other teachers had at least attained the initial level of black belt (there are several levels, and Bobbie now has her second level) before declaring themselves competent to teach others.

Bobbie decided in the end that being the best karate athlete was not so important as having a defined niche, having business sense, and, most important, having the gumption to try it. The point: you don't have to be the best in your field of expertise to be successful in a lifestyle business based on that field. Competence is essential to be sure, but it is a fallacy to assume that only those recognized by the profession as being the best in a field are the only ones who can run a successful business in that field.

Many professionals rightly think in terms of awards, recognitions, and honors as the road to career advancements. These kinds of résumé credits are indeed used to separate and rank job applicants; those with better résumés do tend to have better job prospects. But your résumé is decidedly less important (though certainly not unimportant) when you're on your own and trying to attract clients. The skills needed to run your own business are as important as the technical skills needed to perform the service you're offering. This concept drives some people crazy. How often have you heard: "I'm a much better architect [or other professional] than he is, so how come he is getting more contracts than I am?" Or "I'm a great social worker with 20 years of experience and several awards and certificates of merit. Yet so many social workers are out on their own making double what I'm making at my job, and they have half my experience." Even worse is this kind of logic: "Sandy is a reasonably good cook, but I'm a better one because I have more experience working for prestige restaurants, and I have better training. She opened a successful catering business, so obviously I could too. I'm going to do just that. People will flock to me because they'll quickly understand that I'm better." Defining yourself as better based on your own criteria of quality (or that of other practitioners in your profession) won't lead to a competitive advantage or to more business.

ENTREPRENEUR PROFILE

The Karate School for Women

I don't think my sister, Bobbie, ever had a real job, at least not one that lasted more than two weeks. Bobbie never questioned the idea that her chosen lifestyle came first and work second. While she was a college student in the early sixties, she collected suede scraps from the floor of a luggage factory and sewed them into pocketbooks that sold very well at the University of Connecticut.

After college she moved to New York and dedicated much of her life to the fledgling women's movement and also took an interest in Tai Kwon Do Karate. Though she continued to make and sell pocketbooks in New York, sales waned, and she needed another income. I suppose others in that situation would have looked for a job but not Bobbie. That wouldn't have fit with her lifestyle.

Instead, she talked a few local organizations (colleges, YMCAs, women's groups) into hiring her to teach karate to women. She did this more or less to test the marketplace's response to the concept of self-defense courses strictly for women. The eventual goal was to rent space and open a private karate school. Her classes were well received, she soon developed a following, and she phased out the classes at the colleges and other organizations, consolidating her teaching into her own school in the heart of Greenwich Village.

Early on, before she earned her black belt, Bobbie was concerned about her qualifications to teach. In New York lots of teachers had their black belt, many of whom had more advanced 3rd and 4th degree black belts. Could Bobbie, as a mere brown belt, be a credible teacher? Skill level in a field is only one part of marketing a service. Promotion and reputation have a lot to do with it too. I think in Bobbie's case, a key variable to success was her identifying a clear niche: women not particularly athletic who wanted to learn to defend themselves on the streets of New York. I think had she just set up to teach karate to anyone interested, she would not have succeeded in the face of more established and more experienced competition.

Bobbie's school became quite popular. She could easily have expanded it by hiring instructors and perhaps opening another location, but she never did that. You see, she had a lot of other things that were important to her, such as the women's movement, travel in South America, friends, and more. She only wanted to run the school part-time and have enough money to support her lifestyle. The traditional entrepreneur might not understand this logic nor would many CPAs or business advisors. But I think if you bought this book and have read this far, you understand her thinking very well.

What Is Better?

Some years ago, American automobile companies had a problem. Japanese cars were taking market share away from the American companies because they were perceived to be of better quality. The solution, of course, was to make better-quality cars. As simple as that might seem, it proved to be quite complicated.

Quality may seem a straightforward concept, but it isn't. In the case of automobiles, different buyers had different ways of defining and evaluating quality. Some buyers would visit a showroom, open a car's door, and slam the door shut, determining quality by the sound of the door's slamming. Some car companies responded to this measure simply enough by adding sound insulation that gave the slamming door a solid thunk sound. Other buyers defined quality by the paint job, reasoning that if a car has a flawless paint job, it must also have flawless mechanicals. Still others had their own methods for determining quality. Is the car with sound deadening a higher-quality vehicle than the car without it?

In marketing terms, quality is largely defined and measured by the subjective perceptions of a target market. For better or worse, your prospective customers may not have the same standards of evaluating quality that those within your own profession do. Doctors who have the respect of their peers are most likely to be those who can make the most accurate diagnoses, consistently prescribe and administer the most effective treatment, or spearhead research that leads to new treatment or new understanding of the human body.

Though it may seem superficial, patients are less aware of the behind-the-scenes intricacies of the medical profession and judge practitioners based largely on bedside manner and the ability and willingness to communicate with patients. If asked, "If you were ill, would you prefer the doctor who could quickly cure your illness but was somewhat gruff or the one who would talk nicely and comfort you but couldn't offer as effective a cure?" few of us would choose the latter. Yet in real life, because we probably wouldn't know which doctor was better equipped to cure our illness, the latter doctor would likely be perceived as the better one.

Those within a professional group are capable of judging another's abilities by that profession's measures. In the eyes of your target market, however, professional skills are only one set of criteria used to evaluate quality and decide with whom to do business. Factors like location and the look and feel of physical facilities have little bearing on members' standing within their profession. The teacher of the year, for example, if chosen by other educators, will probably be chosen on the basis of his or her abilities to motivate and teach. A teacher assigned to a beautifully appointed high-tech classroom that is convenient to major highways would have no advantage over a teacher in an old school that is well off the beaten track. However, in the world of competing for, say, teaching writing skills to corporate managers, the centrally located state-of-the-art classroom would have a compelling advantage over the less convenient and less attractive classroom, even if the latter had a more capable teacher.

This is not to say quality doesn't matter; it does. It *is* to say that there are different conceptions of the keys to quality. In operating your own business, you need to be sensitive to the marketplace definition of quality as well as to your own profession's definition of quality.

The point in short is that knowing how to run a business is as important as knowing how to exercise the skill itself that you are selling to your market. Many wonderful architects, teachers, social workers, and other professionals have been less than successful in running their own businesses, despite their professional abilities. And many less-than-outstanding practitioners in those same professions have done well in business. Of course, the ideal scenario is to be an excellent practitioner and an excellent small business manager.

Your New Colleagues

If you're a social worker working for a hospital or a mental health center, your colleagues are other social workers and perhaps other mental health workers. However, if you are on your own, whether a social worker, musician, electrician, or writer, you have another group of colleagues who have nothing to do with your chosen profession. Many of the concerns and problems you have in your own business are similar to those of other small business owners and private practitioners. If you're a teacher, you may well want to discuss teaching methodologies with another teacher rather than with a musician or a Web developer. But if you're a teacher trying to develop a tutoring business, you'll find more understanding and constructive suggestions from other small business owners when it comes to marketing decisions, business planning, and financial issues. Not only will other business owners have more knowledge of these types of issues but their motivation and their perspective may be more congruent with your own simply because, like you, they have chosen the entrepreneurial path. Although the teacher you taught side by side with for ten years may think you're nuts to leave a secure job with a steady paycheck and great benefits, the self-employed social worker and even the self-employed computer repair guy will have no trouble at all understanding your decision to graduate to self-employment.

Medical librarians are trained to do the same type of research that I do in my medical search business. When I was in training, learning to do this work, nearly all my classmates (and the instructors) were medical librarians. All of them worked either for a hospital library or for a large drug company. None were on their own and none aspired to be self-employed. Even though they make up the only professional group that is knowledgeable in the technical aspects of searching for medical information, I share few of the same concerns as these colleagues. I have a great deal more in common with other business owners and self-employed persons, who understand the trials and tribulations of building a service business.

Summary

Becoming self-employed requires a new mind-set for people who are new to working on their own. You must consider and plan for business success alongside success as defined by your own field of expertise. In keeping with the premise of this book, define success by your own criteria. Once defined, look at your situation as objectively as you can and plan an appropriate strategy to achieve that success.

Along the way, you may well learn that your new colleagues—other small business owners and self-employed people—have more understanding and sound advice to offer than do your colleagues from your own field who are not working on their own.

CHAPTER

4

Great Idea, but Will It Fly? (Up-Front Research)

All too many entrepreneurs get into business ventures that are doomed from the outset. Either there is no market, too much competition, major *barriers to entry* that can't be overcome with available resources, or the entrepreneur himself simply doesn't understand enough about the industry he plans to enter. It amazes me that so many people spend so much time and money getting a business off the ground without first doing the most basic information gathering. This is a case in point:

Three engineers, all with extensive backgrounds in medical instrumentation, decided to go into business. All agreed they could design an innovative machine that could measure problems with blood flow through veins and arteries. Such machines have been around for years, but their device would be easier to use, cheaper, and more reliable. Because their machine would be usable and affordable by small medical practices, it would allow tests to be done in the doctor's office that at that time could only be done in a hospital. This would be more convenient for the patient and more lucrative for the doctor, as he could bill for the test instead of letting the hospital collect the test fees.

The engineers built the machine, successfully tested it, and achieved the requisite FDA approval ahead of schedule. The group approached me for assistance in raising investment funds to market their innovative product. Their plan to raise money seemed reasonable enough; they would find about 20 physicians who would each invest between $10,000 and $20,000.

Before getting involved in a project like this, I always do a little evaluation of the marketability of the product or service being launched. To this end, my first step was to take the young company's brochure to a cardiologist friend of mine to ask his opinion of the device. His reaction at first seemed quite positive: "If this machine can do what they say it can, it's quite an accomplishment." It looked good so far.

I next asked the most important question from the point of view of launching a product: "Would you buy one?" His answer came without hesitation: "I doubt it." He then explained that the kinds of disorders for which this machine could test are relatively rare. He said he sees no more than four people a year who would be good candidates on which to use this device and he guessed that his two partners see about the same number. He went on to explain that the test would generally be given to a patient once only, unlike medical tests that are given repeatedly.

To recover the $13,000 cost of purchase over two years (ignoring for the moment interest, maintenance, and other costs) would mean that each of the estimated 12 patients would have to be charged almost $550 for one test.

The doctor also explained that most patients who need the kinds of tests this machine would perform are elderly. Because most elderly persons in this country are covered by Medicare, the doctor's fee for the test would essentially be dictated by Medicare. My next step was to check with Medicare about rates paid for the types of tests this device could perform. The average amount that Medicare pays for these tests is $125, meaning that for this three-doctor practice, the machine would yield about $1,500 per year ($125 × 12 patients). Based on the $13,000 price tag, it simply wouldn't be a worthwhile investment.

Finally, I asked the doctor if there were any type of medical specialist that would have significantly more use for the machine than he did. When he answered no, I knew that this technological breakthrough would be an economic failure.

The engineers had made a typical entrepreneurial mistake. Rather than investigate whether a viable market existed, they merely assumed that one did. It would not have been difficult for them to do the same kind of delving that I did. Had they spent a few hours investigating the device's prospects from a market, rather than a technological, perspective, they could have saved themselves 18 months of work and more than $50,000.

Up-front research is important for any new business and essential for one that involves anything new or different. In the case of some more traditional businesses, the research method may be well established and straightforward. For example, to determine whether to locate a new convenience store in a given area, the research largely involves checking traffic flow, competition, and perhaps readily available neighborhood demographics.

In the case of something innovative, however, you need to at least get an indication that the world (more accurately your target niche) is interested in the product or service on which you propose to base your business. The fact that you may think it's a good idea, or your wife or brother or friend thinks it's a good idea, doesn't mean it's marketable. And just because no one else is already producing it doesn't mean it's marketable. In fact, if no one else is already engaged in a similar business, a good question might be Why not? Could it be that several have tried and learned the concept just doesn't fly? Could it be that no one else has thought of it? A littler digging into the reasons would be well worthwhile.

To many lifestyle entrepreneurs, doing something new and unique is an important reason for going into business. This is laudable to be sure, but keep in mind that the traditional entrepreneur has no such requirement. Copying the working model for a convenience store, print shop, or any of thousands of existing concepts is fine with most small business people. That is why franchise businesses are so successful—their pitch essentially involves duplication of a model that is already proven to work, not uniqueness, creativity, or self-expression. Starting a business based on a concept that is in any way new or unique is starting with an added challenge.

Even if a service exists that your target market clearly needs, that fact alone still may not be good enough to assure a successful business venture. Those in your target market have to *know* they need the product or be ready to be *persuaded* that they need it. Unless enough prospects are ready, willing, and able to become buyers of your product or service, and unless you can reach those prospects without unreasonable effort, you don't have a viable business.

At some point you'll have to make the go/no-go decision and in all likelihood with less than perfect information. Very seldom can entrepreneurs know for certain that their venture will succeed. However, you can and should take several steps to minimize your risk by evaluating your prospects for success before you begin your business. Some of those steps are explained below.

Guerilla Research: The Direct Approach

A client wanted my advice about his idea for a new business venture after he had just sold his company that honed precision machine tools. His new idea involved sharpening scissors for hairdressers. I told him I had no idea whether such a business could succeed, but I could show him what he needed to do to find out.

I advised him to do the following:

- Find out who the competitors were and how their businesses operated. To do this, I advised him to examine periodicals and Web sites that were targeted specifically to hairdressers, looking for ads for sharpening scissors, and to perhaps attend a trade show or two for hairdressers.

- Offer his services to hairdressers on a trial basis. He had already developed a portable machine he could take with him and sharpen scissors in a beauty shop. Much could be learned by actually taking the machine around to beauty shops and trying to sell his services.

This research and trial set him on the road to a very successful business. From ads in trade periodicals he learned he had a number of competitors, but, clearly, there was a market for sharpening scissors for hairdressers. Nearly all of his potential competitors operated by mail order. Scissors were sent to them and returned one to two weeks later. By sending scissors himself to these companies for sharpening, he also learned that quality and turnaround time varied greatly.

From actually trying to sell his services, he learned that hairdressers were very receptive once they could be convinced he wouldn't damage their scissors. Many had sent expensive scissors (professional scissors can easily cost $150 a pair) to a sharpening company only to have them unusable when returned. He solved this concern by offering on-the-spot replacement of any scissors that he damaged.

Finally, he learned that hairdressers love scissors. "Showing a group of hairdressers a display of professional scissors is like showing a group of kids a display of candy bars," he told me. He decided to add scissor sales to his business and today runs a lucrative business with nearly 50 percent of his profits coming from sales rather than sharpening.

Similarly, I was once approached by a talented cabinetmaker who had a prototype for a new product: essentially, a wooden under-the-bed storage device. His concept was to sell it through unpainted furniture shops, which would then resell it to consumers. He was advised that he needed marketing research to determine whether the product could be successfully marketed this way, and he wanted to know what I would charge to do that research. I applauded his desire to limit his risk through up-front research, but I knew a better way than hiring me to ask questions and crunch numbers.

I advised him to spend a few hundred dollars printing business cards and order forms. Next, I suggested that he assemble a few more prototypes to demonstrate the device. Finally, I advised that he put the prototypes into his van (along with the cards, order forms, and a list of unpainted furniture stores) and spend a few days visiting several stores to pitch his product to them. Returning with a pile of orders would be a better indicator than any amount of academic market research. In fact, if he came back with no orders—even if not the outcome, he hoped for—the exercise would still have been great research carried out inexpensively.

This kind of direct approach—asking for and getting (or not getting) orders—adroitly bypasses a lot of academic research. It's not only more accurate in a practical sense, but it's cheaper and quicker. Professional researchers may scoff at this method, arguing that they can provide more comprehensive and scientifically valid data, but for the lifestyle entrepreneur, it is the most efficient and economical way to make the go or no-go decision. Seeking orders in advance isn't always feasible. You can't take orders in a restaurant until you have a kitchen, food, tables, chairs, and so on. In other cases though, there are no obstacles to taking orders in advance of making a major investment. Doing so is a great, low-risk way to test your business concept.

The bottom line is quite simple. Never lose sight of the reality that a business starts with a customer by getting overly caught up in research. Instead, put your initial efforts into figuring out what you need to do to get your first customer and then to get many more to follow that first one.

What Do You Want to Find Out?

Examining data that may indicate prospects for your business success is important, but it's easy to become overinvolved in research and lose sight of your reason for examining that data in the first place. Your reason is to get an indication that you are or are not on the right track and to perhaps modify that track based on the data. Don't fall into the trap of overanalyzing the minutiae of charts and graphs merely for the sake of doing research. Such data won't answer all your questions. Once you've gleaned from it whatever information you can that is relevant to your venture, the rest is academic and not productive from a lifestyle business point of view.

To avoid the seductive trap of research for research's sake, it is best to focus on a few clearly defined questions covering exactly what information you're after. Examples are found in the titles of the following five sections.

Are There Legal or Other Governmental Restrictions?

This question is as straightforward as it is essential. If your business concept is to set up a wine-tasting business in a town that prohibits serving alcohol for all commercial purposes, you don't need to spend time on more research of that concept until you find a different venue. Similarly, if you plan to consult on alternative medicine in a state that requires a medical license for this type of consulting, you don't need to go further unless you have that credential.

A call to your attorney would be a good step to avoid legal obstacles. In many cases, you'll get an immediate green light (and you hope a very small bill, if any). In other instances, your attorney may have to do some checking. If you're reluctant to pay a lawyer, you can contact your state's department of business regulation to find out if there are legal restrictions that apply in your case. However, government bureaucrats tend to focus narrowly on the issue at hand; it is not their job to seek alternative approaches nor seek solutions to your problem. Unless you ask precisely the right questions, you may not get the right answers. Further, the state's personnel may not advise you (or may not know) about county or municipal restrictions that could be obstacles. If your research reveals any questions at all about legal obstacles, then you absolutely must consult an attorney; the money spent for a brief consultation may save a great deal more money and aggravation in the long run.

Is There a Market Niche?

Far too many entrepreneurs just assume that because they think their particular product is a good idea, people out there will buy that product. Once I was approached by a guy who had a design for a pedal-driven rocking horse contraption, and he wanted advice for marketing it. Being a bit skeptical about the prospects for this device in the marketplace, I asked him who he thought would be interested in buying this toy. His response: "Who wouldn't be?" Clearly, as enamored with the device as he may have been, he hadn't defined or evaluated his market niche.

The direct approach (going out and trying to get orders) probably would not have worked for him. He had a design on a drawing board, not a product for which he could take orders. Perhaps he could have talked to a few buyers at toy retail stores to get an idea of the product's prospects. In any case, he should have determined there was a market niche looking for a toy like this before trying to market it.

In many lifestyle ventures, an indication of a niche is established because people seek out a product or service but can't readily find it. Then they talk to others and learn that many of them, too, have sought out a similar product or service only to have encountered the same difficulty. At that point, the proverbial little light bulb goes off, and one person takes the first step toward entrepreneurship. He didn't start off by saying, "Now I'm going to do some up-front research," but that is exactly what he did.

The more assurance you have that a niche for your concept exists, the lower your risk of a frustrating business failure. This chapter has some suggestions for discovering whether your niche truly exists. Once again, the most you can hope for is a good indication that a market niche exists; you won't find any guarantees.

Is There Room for Me within the Market Niche?

Suppose your concept is to teach self-defense to young children. And then suppose you talk to parents of young children and learn that several would be interested in having their children take self-defense lessons. So far, so good. Your next step is to find out whether the niche is crowded with competition or whether there is adequate room for a new competitor. This may well come down to a judgment call of whether you can compete effectively within the niche, but you need information about your competition to make this decision rationally. Examining your competition is discussed later in this chapter.

Can You Get Your Message to Your Niche at Reasonable Cost?

Many entrepreneurs tell me that if they only had better marketing, their business would take off. In many of those cases, this may be true, but there is no way to wave a magic wand and achieve better marketing. Marketing is one of the challenges in making a business successful, and a key factor to be considered is marketing cost. Sometimes, unfortunately, there are no cost-effective ways to reach a market niche. On the other hand, marketing channels do exist in some situations at reasonable cost and other situations exist in which creative modes of marketing can effectively get the message to the marketplace with minimal or no cost. Part of your up-front research requires an honest assessment of your marketing options and the projected costs of those options. (Marketing and promotion are discussed in more detail in Chapter 5.)

Is There an Indication That Profitability Can Be Achieved?

This, of course, is the real question. Chances are that if a market has room for you as a new competitor, and you have an economical way to get the message to your target market, you have a fighting chance of running your business successfully. However, there are exceptions. Say, for example, you're a Web site developer in a community where there are talented college students willing and able to work for very low compensation; this would lower your chance of operating at a reasonable profit.

The rest of this chapter deals with three broad areas that your up-front research should explore. First, I briefly cover the issue of barriers to entry. Next, I discuss researching your market using published data and the Internet and then evaluating your research. Finally, I detail how to research your competition.

Barriers to Entry

Some industries are easier than others for newcomers to break into, especially true for lifestyle entrepreneurs. To set up a business as a Web developer, for example, requirements are not complicated or expensive. Besides the skills to make Web sites, you need a computer and some basic peripherals, Internet access, a telephone, and perhaps stationery. At the other end of the spectrum, if you wanted to set up a new national overnight package delivery service, you would be faced with daunting barriers. You would need planes, trucks, pilots, drivers, representatives in several locations, and so on. Whereas the Web developer could probably get started for under $1,000 (assuming he already owned the computer), the overnight delivery service would require millions of dollars on day one and would have to secure hundreds of thousands of customers very quickly to survive.

In addition to money, other barriers to entry may include licensing requirements (some businesses require them, but most don't) and technical expertise inherent to some industries. Common barriers to entry in some, but not all, industries are customers that are more or less locked in to their current supplier. In other industries, customers are far more fickle and are ready and willing to consider someone new. For example, people are often ready to try a new restaurant but won't readily change the company that delivers their home heating oil.

In the case of lifestyle entrepreneurs, other barriers to entry might be anything that interferes with the nonbusiness aspects of your chosen lifestyle. The necessity of working on Sundays, for example, might not be a significant barrier to entry for the traditional entrepreneur but might be for someone going into business in part to have weekends free.

Make sure you choose a business that has low barriers to entry or at least no barriers that would be incompatible with your lifestyle. In general, service businesses have relatively low barriers to entry as do retail businesses and many Internet-based businesses. Some service businesses, on the other hand, require licensure or certification that can be major barriers for anyone without the appropriate credentials. Fields like medicine and mental health require licensure to practice and have the additional barrier to entry of certification by insurance companies and other third-party payers.

In some situations, government authorities purposely limit the number of businesses of a certain type by requiring permits of which there are only a prescribed number available. In some cities (most notably New York), you can't operate a taxi independently without a medallion, of which only a limited number are available, and availability is strictly controlled by government regulation to allow the city to control the number of cabs on the street. Similarly, permits to serve alcohol in most jurisdictions are only available in a limited number as decided by the city or other governing authority.

A more detailed discussion of barriers to entry is made in Chapter 5.

Researching Your Market Niche

As I've tried to make clear, the best way to establish whether there's a viable market for your product or service is to try to get orders. Later parts of this chapter explain some traditional research-based methods for determining whether a market exists, but a fistful of orders outmaneuvers all those methods. You're far better off with orders and a research study saying it won't work than you are with a research study saying it will work but no paying customers.

Large businesses have several advantages over smaller ones, but an advantage many small businesses have over large ones is their owners' ability to readily do direct testing, such as the kind I advised the scissors sharpener and the cabinetmaker to do. Testing by most larger enterprises needs to be more sophisticated and complex (though not necessarily more accurate). Large companies can't justify sending a guy out with a sample and an order pad to see if a product will fly. Myriad complexities, such as the raw material supply, the organization of management, effect on sales of other products, company image, and long-term strategies, have to be considered and planned for before any testing can be carried out. But the lone entrepreneur or small company owner doesn't have to worry about these sorts of things, at least not in the same way. Most of the details of supply, management, strategy, and the like can be evaluated based on the needs and wants of the entrepreneur, not on the evaluation of myriad influences in other areas.

Even though I have made the case that the best research is to actually attempt to get orders, I recognize that may not be possible in all circumstances. I also recognize that test results of this nature are not always black and white but often gray—somewhere in the middle. That is, you may get some orders, enough to convince you that your concept may be viable but not enough orders to declare it a definite *go*.

If you can and do try to get orders and you get enough to indicate that your business concept will work, you can stop researching and start putting your business together. I purposely used the word *indicate* because that's the most you can reasonably hope for. You will seldom have a guarantee that your business will succeed. Conversely, if you try to get orders but come up empty-handed after many attempts, you can reasonably conclude that your business concept is not viable (at least not without significant adjustment).

If you can't possibly seek orders without setting up your business first, or if your order-taking attempts put you in that gray area, then other (more traditional) research steps might be in order.

The rest of this section outlines some relatively straightforward research steps you can take to get an idea whether your product or service might be viable. Of course, this is not meant to be a complete overview of market research but only an outline of some of the easiest and cheapest steps you can take. In most instances involving a lifestyle business, it is less costly to take some of the basic steps explained below, set up your business, and try making a go of it than it is to hire a professional market researcher.

Using Published Data

A huge amount of data collected by government agencies, business organizations, and academic institutions is available to the public. Although these kinds of data are general in applying to large groups, such as entire industries or entire towns, they can provide valuable insights for business decision making. Because much of these data are obtainable at minimal or no charge, there is hardly a downside to taking a look at the information available to you.

Here are some steps you can take to examine the prospects for your business concept by looking at readily available information.

Statistics and demographics. Traditional advice to entrepreneurs is to examine demographic and statistical information in evaluating a business opportunity. In my opinion, that is a worthwhile step, but it is generally a bit more academic than it is practical. Demographic statistics by definition are derived from very large groups and are general in nature. Such statistics can be misleading and even invalid when applied to a lifestyle business situation. Remember, small business success largely depends on finding and meeting the needs of a particular niche. If the demographics of your city indicate that the number of children aged 6 to 12 is in decline, and statistics also indicate that parents are increasingly likely to look to the Internet and catalog shopping to buy clothing for their children, one may conclude that opening a neighborhood children's clothing store is a bad idea. However, if your niche is perhaps exclusively children's cotton clothing not readily available from mass merchants, and parents at your kid's day care center and play group are complaining they can't find cotton clothing for their kids, the broad statistics found in demographic profiles may not matter in your case. The data derived from informally polling the day care center or play group might well be the better indicator of your business prospects.

In my work of selling businesses, I'm often entertained by novice buyers who study statistics and make projections and decisions about a business for sale based on those statistics. I hear proclamations such as, "Well, according to the U.S. Department of Commerce, sales of printing services are in decline as the country moves toward paperless communications, so I'm going to pass on this forms printing company." This may sound logical in the most general sense. A professional buyer of businesses, however, might look briefly at the statistics, then look at the business itself, and say, "Gee, sales have been going up at about 6 percent each year for this company, and it has 2,100 repeat customers that have been customers for an average of four years. Paperless society or no, people will be using business forms for a long time to come, so the base of repeat customers and the steady increase in sales are more important to me than the Department of Commerce statistics."

Demographic and other statistical data have their place. My warning is to avoid overreliance on such information as it is by nature broadly based and should be only one factor in making decisions for a niche business—and virtually all lifestyle businesses are niche businesses.

My warnings notwithstanding, there are a number of excellent sources for demographic information. Here are a few of them.

- *Local chambers of commerce.* Your local chamber of commerce is responsible for providing resources for local businesses, prospective businesses new to the local area, and existing businesses considering locating a facility in your area. Granted that the role of chambers of commerce is primarily to attract large companies to a community, they nevertheless usually compile local demographic information they will make available to you for the asking. Such information is usually free or almost free and well worth taking a look at.

- *Departments of economic development.* Most states and some counties and municipalities maintain departments of economic development whose functions involve collecting several kinds of statistical data that can be helpful in your preliminary information gathering. Rather than approaching a government economic development office with a request for information about starting a business, a better approach is to ask for specific information, such as demographic information for ABC County or population trends for various cities. Better still, ask for a list of available information reports, and pick carefully from that list.

- *U.S. Industry & Trade Outlook.* The U.S Department of Commerce publishes this annual guide that includes analyses and forecasts for several hundred industries. It outlines the challenges and opportunities faced by various industries and includes many informative charts and graphs. This publication is available at many major libraries. You can also buy the whole guide (in hard copy or on a CD) or buy individual chapters for the various industries covered at <www.ntis.gov/product/industry-trade.htm>.

The same warning holds: This guide is useful for an overall macroview of an industry, but you shouldn't base your go/no-go decision entirely on broad industry data like these.

Researching via the Internet

Thanks to the Internet, a good deal of preliminary research can be done cheaply and easily. The quality of information that just a few years ago would have required major libraries and weeks of time can now be done from your own computer in a few hours. Some of the ways the Internet can be used for start-up research include specific Web sites and newsgroups.

Examining Web Sites of Related Companies

A logical first step in considering a new business venture, especially if it is a bit off the beaten path, is a purposeful search of the World Wide Web. Unless your concept is so unusual that almost no one is running a business anything like it, several Web sites dedicated to your concept can be found. In fact, the number of sites that are promoting your type of business in and of itself tells you something about the validity of the concept and the level of competition.

From these Web sites you can glean a great deal of information, including pricing and marketing technique. You can even get an idea of your relative competitive strengths and weaknesses. Try to read between the lines a bit. For example, are the sites maintained regularly or do several appear as if they haven't been updated for months? Chances are sites that are getting a flow of orders are being maintained in an effort to keep those orders flowing. A site not being maintained (spelling errors, broken links, references to upcoming events for dates that passed months before) indicates that few customers are visiting, so the owner probably lost interest in the site. If there is some sort of hit counter on the site, check it out to see if it's getting lots of hits or very few.

A warning: There is always a temptation to discover exactly what one wants to discover from research, and Web research is no exception. Try not to mold the data to meet the desired conclusion. To avoid this trap, it's a good idea to go into your Web research with a clear idea of the information you're looking for. List specific issues and questions, and search for the answers to those questions, such as:

- How many Web sites come up in a search engine when using terms related to your business concept?
- What is the quality level of each site?
- To what degree is each site maintained (are there broken links, indications of no maintenance for a long time, etc.)?
- Is there any indication of the number of visitors each site is getting (site counters)?
- How do they price their product or service?

Newsgroups

The Web is so popular that it is often incorrectly used as a synonym for the Internet itself, but Internet newsgroups predate the Web. Though they lack the pizzazz of the Web, they do get a great deal of usage and they can be a valuable resource for researching your business concept.

Newsgroups, sometimes called Usenet groups, are electronic discussion forums where users can send and receive announcements and messages revolving around a shared area of interest. Many of these groups are very narrowly focused on a topic or subtopic. For example, there are groups that revolve around cancer, to be sure, but there are also groups that revolve around specific kinds of cancer and specific types and aspects of the disease, such as breast cancer, prostate cancer, alternative treatments, emotional aspects, and the like. Discussion in these groups is not live. People post questions and comments, and others respond to them at their own convenience, which could be minutes or days later.

Because of so many millions of Internet users worldwide, even the narrowest topics attract lots of people to these online discussions. So if you are targeting a particular niche for your business, chances are you can find a newsgroup that revolves around, or at least peripherally deals with, the same concept as your chosen niche. Once you do, it is worthwhile to watch the back and forth for several days to get a handle on the kinds of interests and issues these people—your niche market—discuss. Try to determine what the recurring themes of the discussions are and whether your product or service can solve any of the kinds of problems being discussed.

After you've watched the flow of discussions for a while, go ahead and jump in with your own questions and comments, geared, of course, to checking out your business idea. As these groups are noncommercial and, in fact, sometimes eschew any kind of commercialism, be very careful about offering to sell anything or pitching your business in your newsgroup postings. However, tactfully researching your business concept should be acceptable. If, for example, you're trying to learn about the prospects for your business of evaluating religious artifacts, don't enter a religion newsgroup and ask if anyone wants to hire your services. However, it would be okay to post a question asking "Where can I find reliable specialists who can evaluate certain religious artifacts?" Getting back several posts with dozens of recommendations tells you there is a good deal of demand for this service, albeit with a good deal of competition. Getting several posts saying essentially, "I've been searching for that sort of thing for months and haven't found anyone," tells you something else: there is a need for this service and perhaps a shortage of people fulfilling this need. That, of course, would be an encouraging finding.

If you've never accessed a newsgroup, an easy way to get started is to go to <www.google.com>. Instead of entering a search term in the search box, click the link on top of the search box that says "groups." From there you can search for newsgroups that deal with your area of interest.

Set Up a Test Web Site

The Web can be a cost-effective way to do initial direct testing, a sort of high-tech method to do the kind of testing I advised the cabinetmaker and scissors sharpener to do—try to get orders. Not only can initial testing help you make the go/no-go decision, it can also help you make adjustments in the execution of your concept if you decide that it's a go. For example, if you vary your message, you might learn which messages your target market responds to and which it doesn't. If you test different prices, you might learn where the appropriate price points are. You can, depending on the product or service, vary all sorts of things for testing purposes to get a handle on how best to market it. Even though you can do all this using methods other than the Web, few offer the flexibility and low cost that this medium offers.

Before the Web, test marketing possibilities for very small companies were limited. As I suggested, trying to get orders by most other methods required an investment in time or money or most likely both. In some cases, it may not be feasible to seek

Getting Noticed by the Search Engines

Once upon a time, getting listed in Internet search engines was free and being listed in the top 20 for a given search was relatively easy. In some cases, it was as simple as repeating a key word or search term over and over again. If you were selling cupolas and you used the term *cupola* 100 times on your site, you would appear above the site that repeated it 90 times and so on in a search for cupolas.

Times have changed. Not surprisingly, search engines are finding ways to charge, especially for premium listings—those listings near the top for any particular search term. However, it is still possible to get a free listing and decent (if not top) placement, especially for unusual niche products and services.

The major search engines (Google, Alta Vista) and search directories (Yahoo!) change their placement strategies regularly, but here are some basic principles that seem to work at this writing:

- *Titles and headings.* Words or phrases used in headings on a Web page seem to help in getting listed closer to the top. The Web page title bar, which appears in the bar at the top of a Web page, seems to count even more in the determination of search engine placement. So if you're rehabilitating cupolas, choose a title like "Rehabilitating Cupolas," and use the same term in at least one heading.
- *URL (Web address).* Your key word in the uniform resource locator (URL) can help. If you are selling cupolas, the URL <www.cupolas.com> would help to get good placement (it's taken). If you were rehabilitating cupolas, the URL <www.rehabilitating-cupolas.com> would be great. Search engines don't seem to know how to parse words in the URL, so <www.rehabilitatingcupolas.com> (without the dash) probably wouldn't be as good in attracting search engine attention.

- *Repetition.* It's been a while since simple repetition of key words or phrases passed the search engines' algorithms for gaining good placement. In context, however, repetition does help. That is, if you're selling camping equipment and your title and/or headings contain that phrase, you better have terms like *tent, sleeping bag,* and *lantern* on the page too. If you do, repeating the term *camping equipment* a few times may help.

One thing that clearly helps in search engine placement but is less controllable by a Web designer is the number of inbound links a site has. If your site has 100 other sites linking to it, it will boost your placement significantly.

In the case of Yahoo!, you have to register your site. Most search engines use Internet robots to search out sites and feed the data back to a program that decides whether and where to place each new site it finds. Yahoo!, technically a search directory, uses humans to look at each site submitted and decide its inclusion and placement. You can learn about registering with Yahoo! on its home page <www.yahoo.com>. Though the procedure may change, at this book's press time, you would go to the very bottom of the page and click on "how to suggest a site."

Finally, paying for placement may not be a bad promotion investment. The search engine <www.overture.com> bases placement rankings strictly on the amount someone is willing to pay. That is, if you choose the search term "cupola" and bid 50 cents per click through (anytime someone searches on the word *cupola* and clicks through to your site), you will be ahead of the company bidding 49 cents; it will be ahead of the company bidding 48 cents, and so on. Based on a deal with Yahoo!, the top three bidders for every term also come up in the top three in a search for the same term on Yahoo!.

The search engines have gotten progressively more sophisticated in how their placements are done and are clearly moving away from offering their services free of charge. Nevertheless, they still offer low-cost promotions for companies selling niche products and services.

orders until the business is more fully set up. In cases where trying to sell your product or service is feasible, the Web offers a relatively cheap method for small businesses to test a concept by setting up a Web site and offering a product or service for sale.

Unfortunately, setting up a Web site doesn't guarantee prospects will visit that site. However, the narrower your niche, the easier it is to get decent search engine placement simply because there is less competition for unusual niches. If you specialize in rehabilitating cupolas, you can conceivably get your site to be listed in the top 20 on several search engines when someone types in " rehabilitating cupolas" in a search engine.

You can also discretely promote your site through newsgroups, remembering the noncommercial culture of these groups. Promoting your site in other ways can give you an indication of how much expense and effort it takes to get prospects to visit. With commercial Web site hosting, you typically get some sort of package that reports statistics about visitors to your site, often broken down by pages visited. If you, for example, advertise your site in a newsletter and see your site traffic triple when the newsletter comes out, you know the ad (and the concept) is attracting attention. Of course, turning that attention into orders is better still.

Evaluating Research Results

Before beginning any marketing test, it is important to clearly set your evaluation criteria. Earlier in this chapter, I advised you to carefully define the questions you are trying to answer through your research (see "What Do You Want to Find Out?"). A big part of the evaluation phase involves determining whether the answers you found to your research questions indicate a green light for your business. If you've learned there are insurmountable legal obstacles, your research doesn't have to go any further—that's a glaring red light. However, it is more likely that at first look you may have more of a yellow, proceed-with-caution light, so you'll have to carefully evaluate your findings and make an information-based decision.

If you initially set out to establish whether there is interest in your concept, what did your research show? Is there clear and enthusiastic interest; is there some interest but not an overwhelming amount, and so on? Perhaps you went to the next step and tried to determine the *price point* at which there would be interest. Will people pay enough for your product or service to enable you to earn the amount of money you need to earn?

How about barriers to entry? Is the deck stacked against newcomers, or is it easy to enter the market niche as you've conceived it? Do others already have a significant advantage, such as exclusive agreements with suppliers or an in with your potential prospects that would make competing too difficult? For example, an established piano teacher who is well connected with the music departments of area schools has an advantage that amounts to a barrier to entry, though perhaps not an insurmountable one.

Be careful. There is a tendency to look at research results through rose-colored glasses and see what you want to see. It is important to evaluate the results as objectively as possible to avoid, or to at least minimize, bias. This is why it's best to set your evaluation criteria in advance. Suppose you are considering offering self-defense classes for children. You may have decided in advance that if at least 40 percent of the people you query express strong interest, you've got a good shot of making a go of this business. It will be a lot harder to convince yourself that a 20 percent positive response is pretty good if you've already decided double that is minimally acceptable.

An important difference I see in people who run larger companies, including those who consider themselves professional managers, and those running smaller companies is their level of objectivity in evaluating marketplace data. Most of the people running large companies can separate what they want to see from what they really see. Understandably, lifestyle entrepreneurs who are emotionally invested in a business that is also a lifestyle choice or statement have difficulty making this separation.

Once again, research, especially the informal type that I advocate, will most likely provide less-than-clear answers. It will, however, provide hints and indications of your prospects for success, thereby lowering your up-front risk. With the exception of straightforward issues like required licenses and legal obstacles, the main goal of the kind of research I have outlined here is to gather data in order to make a reasoned go/no-go decision. You will never be 100 percent certain of success, but the closer you can get to that impossible level of certainty, the better. You have to accept some risk in any business venture. The best way to lower that risk early on is to test the concept honestly. And there is no better indication of likely success than securing sales at a good profit margin.

Researching Your Competition

Business competition is a tenet of a free market economy. This tenet applies to each and every lifestyle entrepreneur just as it does to the largest public company. Large company management understands that competition is a fact of business life. They coolly analyze competition in terms of strengths, weaknesses, and opportunities and typically deal with it on a strategic and nonemotionally charged basis. Some entrepreneurs are equally as accepting of the realities of free market competition and deal with it in the same calculating and nonemotional manner. Others, however, react more with emotion than reason and do so on a spectrum ranging from an obsession with crushing their competitors to denying that they even have such a thing as competition. Both of these attitudes are out of perspective and can be damaging to the prospects of a new (or not so new) business. Putting too much time and too many resources into battling the competition drains those resources from other areas.

Pretending there is no competition makes your business more vulnerable to that competition than need be. Further, it denies you the opportunity to learn from your competition.

The following section provides an overview of the need to recognize and define your competition, to learn about it (and learn from it), and to effectively deal with competition without being consumed by it.

Who Is Your Competition?

I like to ask entrepreneurs this simple question: "Who is your competition?" Often (too often) I'll get a response like this: "We don't really have any competition." The people telling me this might go on to explain how their service is so much better than everyone else's or how their customers say they won't even consider doing business with any other company.

Several years ago, when I was meeting with the owner of a payroll service company, I asked him who his competitors were. He responded that there were none in the area, which I knew wasn't true, so I asked to see his Yellow Pages directory. I turned to the category "Payroll Preparation Services" and showed him there were five others right in his small town. He was astounded; he really had no idea they existed.

Many professionals bristle at being asked who their competition is. College professors, social workers, architects, and most other highly trained professionals have learned that others in the same field are *colleagues,* not competitors. The concept of competing with your colleagues is somehow unseemly and, well, unprofessional. Make no mistake about it, though—if you are practicing your profession privately, others in your field and in your market area are your competitors.

In business, your competition is just that—your competition. Call it what you want, but anyone who is after the same customers as you are is your competition—they or you, but not both of you, may win that business.

A lot of competition is indirect even though indirect competitors are trying to attract some of the same customers you are. For example, my friend Elaine, who rents apartments to tourists in European cities (see the entrepreneur profile in the next chapter: Apartments in Europe) competes with a few other agents who also rent apartments. Elaine, however, is also competing with hotels, hostels, cruise ships, and anyone else who provides lodging to tourists in those European cities. Even if you think your service is vastly superior to others or so different that in your view it is not the same at all, those offering a service that can be an alternative to yours are your competitors. It is not your perspective here that matters; it is the perspective of potential customers.

Call it by whatever euphemism you please, but you need to have a sense of who your competition is and how they do things in order for you to effectively compete for customers and dollars. The kinds of questions about your competitors you need answered include:

- What do they offer?
- How do they promote their offerings?
- How do they package their offerings?
- How much do they charge?
- What competitive advantages do they have over you?
- What competitive advantages do you have over them?

In regard to the last two questions, I'm not only referring to advantages in terms of product quality or service performance. If a competitor has an advantage in gaining customers, a cost advantage, or a knack for getting media publicity, those are advantages, even if their product or service quality is inferior to your own. Likewise, if they make a better product but you have a cost advantage or have ready access to potential customers, you have important advantages.

For example, suppose you are a great piano teacher setting up a business in the town to which you recently moved. Suppose there is another piano teacher in town who charges more than you do but has far less experience and a reputation that can't hold a candle to yours. But that person is also the music teacher at a large local middle school and has been in that position for the past seven years. She has a built-in advantage over you. Despite her lesser abilities and higher rates, she is known in the community and is in regular touch with potential students (her niche market). Your being new in town without the advantage of those great connections have only your superior skills as an advantage, which sadly puts you at an overall disadvantage, at least for now.

The more you can learn about what your competitors do and how they do it, the better you can position your company to compete with them. If, for example, you learn that the mythical piano teacher who teaches at the middle school is well liked but only accepts private students on Thursdays and Saturdays, your opportunity may be to offer classes on the other days of the week. If you learn that she insists that students come to her house, your opportunity might be to offer lessons at the student's own home.

It's a good idea to look at the various elements of the product your competition is offering, figure out its vulnerabilities—those aspects where you can do better—to gain an advantage. Keep in mind, though, that by doing better, I mean better from the prospective customer's point of view, not yours. If your piano lessons are musically more sophisticated in the eyes of professional musicians, that won't be too helpful in gaining clients if they're looking for convenience and charisma and can't appreciate the sophistication gap. Far too many small business people are frustrated because they can't make the world see that their product or service is *better.* But it is only better because they're relying on *their* definition of better, not on that of their niche market.

Getting Competitive Information

All sorts of methods are available for getting information about your competitors. My general advice is to merely put yourself in the role of a prospective customer making a buy decision. A person considering buying a product or service might look at brochures or other advertising, ask friends who have used that product or service for recommendations, visit a few businesses, make inquiring phone calls, and so on. Of course, not all of these possibilities are available for every business, but the idea is to get information efficiently, not to meticulously follow each possible avenue.

Competitors' advertising. All businesses, regardless of size, have to get word to their target market about their offerings. For many companies, advertising of one sort or another is an important vehicle for getting that word out. Take a close look at what and how your competitors are advertising, and perhaps more important, *where* they are advertising. The what and how offer a glimpse into their purported areas of expertise and overall marketing strategy (do they stress price? convenience? quality?). Where they advertise is a good indicator of the places their target market (and your target market) can be reached. If an established competitor is regularly advertising in a certain publication, you can assume that that publication is successfully reaching its intended target market. Otherwise, the competitor wouldn't waste its marketing dollars there. Likewise, if it is regularly placing flyers in certain areas or delivering coupons in certain neighborhoods, you can assume that those advertising strategies are delivering results and might for you as well.

As noted previously, a company's Web site also offers a good insight into its marketing strategies. In looking at a competitor's Web site, try to determine whether that site is generating business for the competitor. Again, it will take some investigation and estimating because the site won't come right out and say, "We now get 40 percent of our new business from the Web." However, there will be clues, such as whether it is well set up for taking orders and whether it is regularly maintained with updates, current announcements, and the like.

Telephone inquiries. Many business inquiries start with a phone call. If you were considering hiring a lawyer, architect, or piano teacher, a phone call would be a typical first step. For some reason, fledgling entrepreneurs are often reluctant to place a phone call pretending to be a prospective customer. It is a wonderful way to get information simply because it is such a normal step that is unlikely to arouse suspicion. Further, asking all sorts of questions is an expected part of such a phone inquiry. If you're uncomfortable with doing this, get a friend or associate to do it for you.

Try to keep the questions to those that a prospect is likely to ask so as not to arouse suspicion about your true intent in calling. A good strategy would be to ask the most innocuous questions first (When are appointments available? How much does it cost?) and progress toward the more sensitive ones that could arouse suspicion (How's business been for the past few months? Is business growing?). This way, if the person gets suspicious and terminates the conversation, you'll at least have several of your questions answered.

Visit. Other than retail stores, few types of businesses lend themselves to unannounced personal visits. However, if retail is your area of interest, by all means check out those businesses that would be your competitors. Visiting a few will yield a wealth of information, such as pricing, products being carried, merchandising practices (how products are displayed), and more. Sometimes, visiting stores that cater to a niche similar to yours but in a different geographic area can yield new ideas that are not being used in your area yet. In fact, many businesses have started because someone visited a faraway place and discovered business practices that might be successful in their local area. The concept of Starbucks Coffee, as we know it today, took root when Howard Schultz, its current owner, visited the cafes of Italy and decided to try the concept of gourmet coffee shops in the United States.

Many nonretail industries have trade shows where companies display their products to the trade (their target market). If you're planning to sell a product or service to a distinct industry or specific interest group, attending a few trade shows can offer a good overview of the industry, the competition you face, and the opportunities that might await someone from the outside with fresh ideas.

Talking to customers. If you were considering hiring a piano teacher for your child, for example, you might very well talk to a few parents of current and past students. You might try doing the same thing as part of your competitive research. If you can learn who a few of your competitors' customers are, a conversation about what they like and don't like about a particular piano teacher (or Web designer, language tutor, etc.) could be helpful in responding to customer needs in ways your competitors aren't.

Buying their products. To learn about their competitors' latest offerings, automobile manufacturers routinely buy their competitors' cars, test drive them, and take them apart. When I started my medical research business, I bought a report from a competitor and looked for areas where I could do better. There is nothing illegal or unethical about this, and it is a great way to learn about a competitor's product.

Better business bureau (BBB). You can check with your local BBB to find out if there have been any complaints against your competitors. In the unlikely event of a long list of complaints, you are equipped with useful competitive information to use in attracting customers away from a problematic business.

Focus of Research

In research, especially research as highly charged as investigating your competitors, it is tempting to be sidetracked into lots of unproductive directions. Do yourself a favor by staying focused on finding the information you need to find without spending a lot of time on superfluous research. To avoid getting sidetracked, I suggest writing up a brief research plan that clearly states the kind of information you're looking for. This could be a list of questions on a single sheet of paper that you want answered about each competitor, such as:

- How does it charge?
- What are its competitive strengths?
- What are its competitive weaknesses?
- What do customers say about it?
- Where does it advertise?
- What aspects of the business do its ads stress?

Each situation will be different, but these are some typical questions that would be relevant to almost any type of business.

The basic question you're trying to answer is, Is there room for me to compete effectively in the market niche I've chosen? It's okay if you have to modify or reframe your niche a bit as long as you're convinced there is a place for you somewhere within that niche. Be as honest as you can with yourself in answering the question, Why will prospective customers come to me with their business rather than to one of my competitors? It's fine and in fact inevitable that some prospective customers will take some of their business to others. As long as enough prospects become customers of yours so you can make a living, then you have the makings of a successful business.

Competitiveness

When I was in the video production business, I found the business, at least in my geographic area, hotly competitive. Competitors would bad-mouth one another as a matter of course and point out each other's weaknesses (real and contrived). Customers could pit one company against another for lower prices and other concessions. Cooperation between competitors was rare and always approached with trepidation.

I've now been in business brokering for several years. In this business, competition is not a major issue. Business brokers in my market niche close just a few deals a year but earn a sizable commission on each one. We cooperate with one another, sharing lessons learned and even arranging to share commissions in some cases. I feel that as long as I can make a few deals, it's fine that the others make their deals too. Apparently, my competitors see it the same way. Even though selling a company is an arduous project, fraught with pitfalls that could kill a lucrative deal at any time, competition is not one of the major dangers. Seldom do we compete directly with one another to attract a buyer or a seller.

All industries are competitive to some degree. Even in business brokering, I know I would have a much easier time if I were the only broker in my area. Some industries, however, are far more competitive than others, ranging from very friendly to cutthroat. The level of competitiveness should be considered in deciding whether to get involved in a particular industry. If you thrive on competition, you'll be happy in a competitive industry; if you don't, you may not be.

Getting an idea of the degree of competitiveness in an industry is not difficult. Pretending you're a prospective customer, make a few inquiring phone calls to businesses in the industry to ask a about others in the industry. If you hear a litany of terrible practices and offenses committed by competitors, it looks like a cutthroat industry. If you hear only mild negatives (for example, "They're quite good at this type of work, but we're better at doing the work you need"), it indicates a friendlier competition.

Also, examine advertising in the industry. A competitor stressing that it's better than the other competitors indicates a hotly competitive industry. A business stressing what it can do for you (actually for its target market), without mention of the competition, indicates a less competitive situation.

"Beware Stupid Competition"

I once attended a seminar for entrepreneur educators, at which a college professor gave a talk entitled "Beware Stupid Competition." I couldn't resist the title, so I attended. The speaker's premise was that reasonably intelligent competitors understand the dangers in taking drastic and self-defeating steps to compete and understand that competition is a fabric of a free market system. They therefore act rationally and predictably.

Stupid competitors, however, don't think things through. For example, they might cut prices so far that they inevitably lose money or make guarantees that eventually destroy their companies. Such steps might lead to their ruin, but they could easily lead to the ruin of competitors as well. If you're buying widgets for $10, and your competitor at first is doing the same but starts selling them for $9, you're both in trouble. It's incredibly stupid, but neither company can survive for too long in this scenario. A smart competitor may sell a product at a loss for a while, but he'll understand the mathematics well enough to know that he can't continually lose money on every sale in the hope of making it up in volume.

A corollary to this principle might be "Beware Transient Competition." Currently, Web development is a hot field for entrepreneurs, including lifestyle entrepreneurs. The problem is that some college students and even some high school students are as capable as adults twice their age at creating Web sites. However, even though adults might have families and obligations (read expenses), the students might be delighted to work for just enough to buy a new laptop or a plane ticket to the coast.

Such competition is not insurmountable. Sure, some prospective clients will go for the lower-priced student labor, but those who consider responsibility, professionalism, and other factors that come with maturity will look beyond price. As discussed before (and as will be discussed again), it is a matter of defining your niche and catering to that niche. In a case like student competition, don't target the niche that considers low price the key selection criterion.

Once your initial research is completed and assuming a good indication of possible success, your next steps involve determining how you'll gain customers, making financial projections to put your prospects in terms of dollars and cents, and writing a basic business plan. These topics are covered in the following chapters.

CHAPTER

5

Marketing

A business starts with a customer—a truism that seems too obvious to mention. But people lose sight of it, and it deserves mention. It's easier than one would think to be sidetracked with the myriad issues facing a nascent business and forget this most integral ingredient of any company: customers.

By its very definition, customers are obtained through marketing. That's what marketing is: offering a product or service that people want or need, finding those who want or need it, and convincing them to purchase it. As such, marketing is at the very heart of any and every business.

To many people, marketing means advertising and promotion. We often hear of a company's TV advertising campaign referred to as its marketing campaign. Advertising is indeed a part, albeit the most visible part, of marketing; but advertising is only one element of marketing. Marketing is the whole system of getting and keeping customers. In 1985, the Committee on Definitions of the American Marketing Association defined marketing as follows:

> Marketing is the process of planning and executing the conception, pricing, promotion, and distribution of

ideas, goods, and services to create exchanges that satisfy individual and organizational objectives.

A more succinct definition from a marketing text:

> Marketing may be defined briefly as those activities that relate an organization successfully to its environment. (David G. Hughes, *Marketing Management,* Addison-Wesley, 1978.)

The point is that marketing involves a lot more than advertising. It is the entire process of interacting with your market—your customers and prospective customers. In fact, many lifestyle companies, even some fairly large ones do no advertising, yet they still do marketing.

The Four *P*s

If you take an intro to marketing course, you'll learn that marketing is made up of the four *P*s. These four *P*s of marketing are product, price, place, and promotion. Admittedly, a little rewording had to be done to find appropriate words starting with the letter *P,* but this nevertheless does provide a useful way to understand what marketing is about. Let's have a look at those four *P*s.

Product

This is what you are offering to your prospective customers. It could be a tangible product or an intangible service. Ideally, the product (or service) should be designed and offered to respond to the needs of a defined target market. In the old school, a company made a product that it thought it could convince people to buy, then endeavored to sell it through advertising, direct selling, and whatever other method could be employed to get that product sold. The more enlightened new school contends the product should be designed around the needs of its intended market and modified as necessary to better fit those needs. If a company can make a product that its target market both needs *and* knows it needs, the battle is at least half won.

In small business, the product should be tailored to the specific needs of a market niche. Children's clothing that one would buy at a mass merchandiser's facility is not the same product as all-natural 100 percent cotton clothing designed for the marketing niche seeking all-natural children's clothing. The mass merchandiser may well decide that the market for all-cotton clothing is so small that it is hardly worth bothering with. Yet it may be a profitable product for a small business interested in serving a particular niche.

Price

On the surface, price needs no explanation—it's how much you charge for your product or service. It is, however, a bit more involved than that. For example, there is competitive pricing, or pricing to match or beat your competition. This is a common method of pricing that works well for large companies that enjoy economies of scale and high enough volume to make money at a low pricing range. However, competing based on price is generally dangerous for smaller companies that don't enjoy economies of scale. Even though every company must consider pricing to a degree in light of what others are charging, it is best to avoid designing an entire pricing strategy based on underpricing the competition. As a rule, smaller companies have higher costs in producing products, because they can't get the same quantity discounts and economies that large companies can. Neither can small companies afford to temporarily lose money on a particular product or service as large companies can in hopes of gaining market share (or in hopes of putting others out of business).

Don't assume that the lower price automatically attracts more customers. For example, if a new doctor in town put a sign in his window that read "Special: Full Physical Exam only $9.95" or a new dentist advertised "Two cavities filled for the price of one," would you be tempted to visit either of these professionals? Probably not. For some professional services, prospective clients expect that a higher price is an indication of higher ability, and a price well below market rate is met with suspicion. This principle works for tangible products as well. Would you be suspicious of a new gourmet coffee shop selling coffee for 40 cents a cup?

Luxury pricing is a strategy that takes advantage of, for lack of a better term, *snob appeal.* I will argue that in a blind taste test, few vodka drinkers could differentiate between a $12 bottle of vodka, a $15 bottle, or a $20 bottle. Yet I'll bet that even those who miserably misidentify which sip belongs to which bottle and are told they did would still not change their vodka-buying preferences. People draw their identity in part from their indulgences. The same principle holds for jewelry, cars, clothing, and all sorts of other things. Stated simply, some people prefer to pay more to feel they are getting something better. You are better served working to figure out how much your target market is prepared to pay than figuring out the lowest price for which you can afford to sell your product.

Promotion

This is the *P* that is too often thought of as the whole story in marketing—not surprising as this is the stuff that shows. Promotion involves any and every form of getting the word out about your product or service, including the largest-scale methods (such as TV or newspaper advertising) as well as Web sites, direct mail, and slipping flyers under dorm room doors. Though most promotion is paid for, there are exceptions, such as publicity. Journalists hate to see media articles included as an element of promotion, but marketers certainly think of press coverage this way.

Word of mouth is the best advertising of all. In fact, a lot of very expensive advertising is designed as a catalyst for prompting people to talk about a product or service—or even the ad itself. The ads during the Super Bowl fit this latter criterion. A few seconds of Super Bowl advertising costs hundreds of thousands of dollars, but obviously some companies think it's money well spent. Not only is the ad seen by millions of people, but each Super Bowl ad gets lots of press and discussion for days before and after its debut.

Most of us understand that advertising is designed to highlight the advantages and benefits of a product (while ignoring or downplaying the bad), so we view it with a skeptical eye. But when a trusted friend tells you how good a product is or recommends a particular lawyer, consultant, or Web designer, skepticism vanishes. A successful ad may encourage a few people to try a product. Assuming the majority of those who try it like it, they will not only keep buying it but will also recommend it or at least be seen using it, thereby encouraging others to try it. In the perfect textbook scenario, this advertising-trying-recommending sequence keeps replaying and mushrooming and makes the product more and more successful.

I very much believe in promotion as a catalyst for a word-of-mouth advertising approach for lifestyle businesses. Ad budgets are limited (nearly nonexistent in some cases), so those limited budgets need to get maximum bang for the buck. Getting some good word-of-mouth advertising going is about the best bang for your buck you can get. If you're offering collection services to medical offices, perhaps you'll send out 300 letters to area doctors' offices. Those letters may bring you three clients, a return less than stellar. But if two of those three clients each refers another client, and one of those two referred clients refers someone else, now we're looking at a very nice return from those letters.

Place

This *P* had to be rigged to come up with the four *P*s of marketing. I'm actually talking here about *distribution,* which is arguably the least exciting of the four *P*s. Compared to figuring out exactly how your product or service should be designed and how to promote it, moving it to your customers seems mundane and because it is ostensibly mundane, it is overlooked as an area of opportunity (and certainly of excitement) by marketers. Yet there is room for opportunity and creativity here.

There are a few classic examples of companies exploiting creative distribution to score major marketing coups. For example, in the 1950s, Timex boldly decided to sell wristwatches in outlets other than jewelry stores. Although the idea of buying a low-priced watch in a drugstore doesn't seem so radical now, it was groundbreaking then. Without that radical twist in distribution, we may not have had the ubiquitous low-priced watch today.

Another example involves L'eggs panty hose. Panty hose were clothing store and perhaps drugstore products until the late 1960s, when the marketing people for L'eggs reasoned quite correctly that buyers of panty hose were women, and women frequented grocery stores and supermarkets. So why not put the product where the target market will have ready access to it? Well, of course, it proved a great idea, and now buying pantyhose in supermarkets is the accepted norm.

Timex and L'eggs are hardly what we typically consider lifestyle businesses. But a lot of small businesses succeed because they, too, make products more convenient for people. Big business typically relies on regimentation and economies of scale, not on individualized service. A mechanized car wash business, for example, is costly to set up but cheap to run. As long as paying customers drive through at a high-enough rate, this business will make money. Mechanized car washers can do a fairly good job quickly and for a reasonable price, so thousand of car owners use them. Last week I saw in my neighbor's driveway a small truck outfitted to be a mini-car-wash system. The entrepreneur running it had what he claimed was a thriving business washing cars at customers' homes and offices. He did a far more thorough job than the big car wash facilities did (yes, some by hand) and was able to command a lot more money for each job. His whole business was based on a somewhat unusual way of distributing a common service. This is one small business example of exploiting distribution. There are many more, and I bet you can come up with a few that you've seen too.

Marketplace Point of View

Has anyone ever thrown you a sales pitch that fell on (your) deaf ears? I'm talking about one in which nothing the salesperson said about the wonderful features of the product he was selling mattered to you. Perhaps you were inquiring about a laptop computer and cared only about its weight and battery life, but the salesperson went on about RAM, gigabytes, and expansion slots. Or maybe a credit card company telemarketer was pitching a new Visa card to you by talking about low interest rates, but you never carry balances and therefore pay no interest.

In those examples (and countless others) the salesperson is not looking at the product from your point of view. The reason may be that he or she has only one pitch (the credit card company telemarketer probably fits this category) or has misread your needs.

Not everyone has the same needs or the same way of evaluating a product or service. However, people in marketing can be grouped into niches where similarities are based on needs and viewpoints. If the credit card telemarketer was using a list of people who regularly carried credit card balances, she would have been reaching a specific niche and would have had a better chance of her sales pitch being heard. Likewise, the computer salesman's pitch might have been effective for computer aficionados (all right, geeks), but another approach, and probably another computer, would have been more appropriate for the customer looking for a lightweight machine to use exclusively for word processing.

Automobile companies know that any car you buy will get you from point A to point B. They also know that getting from place to place is only one of the reasons that people buy cars, and their choices are made for other reasons. Auto companies do a wonderful job of segmenting the market, dividing it into niches. Some cars are designed and promoted to appeal to the practically minded who are looking for a reliable and sensible vehicle. Other segments of the market are looking for a car to enhance or create a chosen image. For example, the promotion for a car designed to appeal to younger men looking for a cool image might show pretty girls flocking around the car admiring the car and the guy in it. Other car buyers lust after cars based on their speed, power, and performance. The auto companies satisfy this segment with muscle cars shown off through macho ads.

Okay, you're an aspiring self-employed person, not a huge automobile company, so how does *market segmentation* apply to you? Like car companies and almost any successful company, you have to look at your product or service from the point of view of its intended buyer. Unlike the car companies, you'll probably be serving one or maybe two segments. The more you understand how your target market or markets perceive your product; how they evaluate quality, price, and value; and especially how your product meets their needs, the more easily your sales job will be. Many specialized small companies exist only because larger companies didn't understand their target market.

Many large tour operators (American Express and Liberty Travel, for example) do a great job organizing efficient tours with good value. There are also countless special interest groups that want to travel but whose members have different needs and different reasons for traveling than do most travelers. That's why smaller tour operators who understand and can cater to the needs of perhaps Holocaust survivors, cancer patients, or orchid gardeners can flourish. More likely than not, the organizers of these niche tours understand the segment they're serving so intimately because they are part of that segment.

You may be selling Web development services, but your prospective clients are buying something other than a Web site—for example, sales leads, a company image, or a more efficient customer service vehicle. People don't really buy cosmetics; they buy the perceived beautification these chemicals offer and the perceived opportunities and status that beautification affords. People don't buy karate lessons; they buy the security that comes with knowing self-defense.

In my corporate video business, I initially centered my selling pitch around the advertising value of a corporate video. I soon learned that CEO ego was a large part of what I was selling, so I added to my pitch to the CEO (or whoever the "pitchee" was) the question: "Would you be willing to do an on-camera introduction?" Sales went up as did the number of CEO faces on our video and the number of CEO egos that were stroked.

The lesson here is to look at your product or service from the perspective of its intended buyers. What are they really buying and why? Chances are they are buying something a bit different from what you're selling for reasons not exactly what you think they are.

What Should Be versus What Is

When banks introduced automatic teller machines (ATMs) in the late 1970s, the machines proved slow to catch on. The problem wasn't technical; they worked pretty well. The problem had to do with the users or, more precisely, the nonusers. Banks had considerable difficulty convincing customers who always banked with human tellers to instead use a newfangled machine. ATMs had the potential of great convenience for bank customers, if only customers would use them. Banks ran TV ads touting the virtues of ATMs and offered discounts, free gifts, and more in an effort to convince recalcitrant customers to use the new ATMs.

The difficult ATM introduction is but one example that people are slow to accept change despite the clear benefits and advantages of new ways. In the late 1990s, many people were convinced the Internet would make traditional brick-and-mortar retail stores obsolete. After all, Web sites offer a far more convenient and efficient way to buy stuff. You could check out information about various products that you wanted to buy, compare prices, and make buying decisions without salespeople hovering over you. Best of all, you could do it right from your own home, where the goods would be delivered soon after they were ordered. Well, despite their antiquated inefficiencies, traditional retail stores are still here, coexisting with the Internet.

Although it is frustrating to those developing and selling newer and technologically improved solutions, attitudes and ingrained habits are a lot slower to change than is technology. Convincing people to accept change, technological or otherwise, is a difficult undertaking. Long-practiced habits, a formidable foe of better products and better methods, have to be overcome. This is a difficult fact for entrepreneurs to accept. Many entrepreneurs have come up with new and clearly improved products or services only to see the marketplace largely ignore them despite their product's superiority. That something is clearly better doesn't necessarily mean the world will welcome it with open arms. Innovation is not as powerful an agent of change as it perhaps should be.

Convincing large groups of people to make major changes in the way they perceive and do things isn't impossible, however. ATMs are largely accepted now, thanks to the continuing efforts of the banking industry. Far more people use their seat belts now than they did ten years ago, thanks to not only law enforcement penalties but also to government public awareness campaigns. However, getting people to change their habits involves massive (read time-consuming and expensive) effort. For the banking industry or the government or for very large companies, it is conceivably doable if they committed adequate resources.

Seldom can a lone entrepreneur or a small business owner change people's habits on more than a very small scale. Within a small market niche, prompting people to change in significant ways can be very difficult to achieve. It is much easier to work with people's perceptions and habits as they are than it is to try to change them.

This can be an especially difficult concept for entrepreneurs to accept, particularly lifestyle entrepreneurs who want to share a creative expression with the world. Making an improvement or contribution to the world is the reason many of the people to whom this book is addressed want to go into business in the first place. If this is your situation, I recommend introducing your innovation in small steps. Accept the commonly accepted habits of your target market as a restriction that will have to be dealt with. No matter how right you may be or how much better your product is, you won't be able to persuade your target market to throw out its entrenched habits and accepted norms overnight. You might, though, get it to consider small steps away from the tried and true.

My video company was hired to produce a video of a huge trade show for professional architects in the early 1980s, when computer-assisted design (CAD) was just being introduced. The huge exhibit hall was aglow with big-screen monitors demonstrating some very impressive design capabilities that the state-of-the-art software and hardware made possible. Most of the architects looked bewildered, even shocked; these were people who had learned architecture with colored pencils and drafting paper and had practiced with those low-tech materials for 5, 10, or 20 years or more. Now they were faced with incomprehensible machinery that looked as though it came form the set of Star Wars, and they were being told by major companies like IBM that their way of dong things was hopelessly antiquated. To add insult to injury, buying the stuff that they didn't want would cost many thousands of dollars.

Amid the Star Wars machinery was a small company showing a device that used a modest computer and mechanical arms that held colored pencils. As the user created designs, the pencils slowly drew the design on the drafting paper. Compared with the state-of-the-art technology, this device was a joke; the techies running the other demonstration booths made fun of it as a throwback. But lo and behold, it got a great deal of attention from the architects because it was something they could relate to. It used the kinds of pencils and paper they used every day. It involved a whole lot less of the intimidating and incomprehensible technology that others were showing; and the architects could clearly see how the device worked.

This was a perfect example of working within accepted norms and proposing incremental steps forward. The small company that was showing this device knew its target niche well: architects who weren't ready for major technical change but might accept incremental change. Perhaps the bigger companies came away with more business, but this small company did extremely well proportionate to its size and its investment.

Niche Marketing

Most dictionaries define *niche* broadly as a place or position particularly suitable for the person or thing in it. A similar definition, particularly suited to its use in business, is a limited area of demand for a product or service.

Almost every small business that succeeds does so because it services a niche. Niches can take several forms. They can be geographical, such as a convenience store that serves people living in a particular area who want only a few items or to shop during odd hours when bigger stores may not be open. The people shopping in neighborhood convenience stores are aware that they can buy the same items cheaper elsewhere, but they willingly pay a premium for the convenience offered. The convenience store owner doesn't consider the major supermarkets his competition because he understands that there is a place for him—a niche.

A niche can also be, and often is, a grouping according to a particular need. People with cancer certainly form a niche as do special needs students and left-handed people. Each of these groups and thousands of others have specific needs that the vast majority of the population don't have.

In designing your business and marketing strategy, it may well be necessary to sharpen your focus on a particular niche market by clearly differentiating your business from those of your competitors. A new business needs to give people in its target market one or more reasons to consider doing business with it. Just setting up a business isn't enough, especially if the perceived needs of your target market are being adequately met. Differentiation doesn't have to be radical or revolutionary. Lower prices, more flexible hours, or faster service can be adequate differentiations if the target market perceives those attributes to be important and to be lacking by companies currently serving the niche.

Small businesses often differentiate themselves by carving niches out of large groups by catering to specific interests within those groups. My friend Elaine (see entrepreneur profile below: "Apartments in Europe") caters to a very small part of the large European tourist market—those who seek short-stay apartments rather than hotels. Also, my sister found a niche among the group of people who wanted to learn karate—nonathletic women (see Chapter 3). There are businesses that cater to Civil War reenactment buffs and to people who want to feed their pets only organic food. In fact, there is a seemingly endless number of particular subgroups that can be carved from larger groups by homing in on, and catering to, special interests that aren't being adequately served by the mass offerings.

By nature, some niches have to be niches because they are so small that it wouldn't be worthwhile for a larger company to serve them. In fact, there are niches so small that the entire market is large enough for only a few people to earn a living by servicing it. At this writing, I am in the process of brokering the sale of a company that makes a lubricant essential for a popular parking brake cable offered in many U.S.-made cars. The automobile companies have specified this lubricant, and only two companies currently supply it. Any of a hundred chemical companies could make the same product (the specifications detail how it is made) and offer it for sale. However, with total annual sales in the $1 million range, it simply isn't worth it for others to get involved and carve up a tiny market any further. The two companies supplying it have a nice, albeit tiny, niche that is resistant to competition simply because it's so small.

ENTREPRENEUR PROFILE

Apartments in Europe

Elaine Carroll loves to travel. While living in India, she arranged for her husband's English family to send her a selection of European catalogs so she could arrange her next summer's trip to Ireland, Wales, France, Spain, and Portugal. From the catalogs, she selected cottages and apartments in some of Europe's most desirable areas and found her trip to be enormously enjoyable, largely because of her accommodations. Her family loved the extra space and comfort, the privacy, and the increased contact with local people. Elaine and her husband also appreciated the cost savings; they paid much less than they would have for comfortable hotel rooms and in Ireland even had enough room to invite and pamper an elderly uncle for a week.

On returning to the United States, several of Elaine's friends asked how she had arranged such a fabulous trip. And thus the idea for a new business was formed. Elaine started by representing a few select European companies and eventually developed her own portfolio of apartments, cottages, and villas.

Today, through her company Vacation Homes Abroad <www.vacationhomesabroad.com>, she represents rental apartments in Paris, London, Dublin, and Rome and houses in France, Italy, England, and Ireland. She takes several trips a year to these countries to list new properties for rent, talk business with apartment owners and agents, and generally tour the properties to make sure her clients are getting the quality she wants to deliver. And, yes, the travel is fully and legitimately tax deductible.

Though Elaine insists the business isn't always as glamorous as it seems, she admits that she very much enjoys earning a living through her lifestyle business.

Access to Your Niche

Identifying a niche is step one. Once your niche is clearly defined, the next challenge is to be sure you can get access to that niche. If there isn't a clear way to reach your niche with your message, it may as well not exist. This doesn't mean you have to be able to reach every single person or organization within your chosen niche, but it does mean you need to be able to reach enough of its members that you can earn an adequate income by serving that niche.

In our brokering business, my partner and I spend a good deal of time identifying industries ripe for mergers and acquisitions. Our criterion for access to the chosen industry is simple and clear: We have to be able to procure a good mailing list of companies within the industry that includes the name of each company's chief executive or owner, because only the chief executive or owner can make the decision to sell the company. With such a list, we know how to announce our presence and promote ourselves. Without the list, the industry is of little value to us, because we can't contact the people we have to in the way that works for us.

For another example, consider a friend of mine who is a college counselor advising students about college choices. Unlike most college counselors, Sharon specializes in assisting learning disabled students choose, apply to, and get admitted to appropriate colleges. She certainly can't buy a list of learning disabled high school students the way we can buy lists of companies by industry. Nor has she found a publication or other advertising source that reaches her niche. Instead, she keeps in regular contact with a number of high school guidance and college counselors who send her referrals. The high school counselors can deal effectively with most college-bound students, but they are not equipped to deal with the particular niche that my friend deals with, so they gladly refer those students to her.

The Internet has been a great help in accessing niches that were previously difficult to reach. A business like Sharon's college counseling service might do well reaching its niche through a Web site. A list of learning disabled high school students may not be available but a lot of students and parents may be going to search engines and inputting "college and learning disabilities" in hopes of finding someone just like Sharon. Many niches that were once not feasible as businesses because getting access to an adequate number of prospects was too difficult may now be feasible because of the Web. If the need is pressing enough and the product or service is difficult to find, people will search for it on the Internet and will do so in increasing numbers in the future. For this reason, the Web is also a great way to test a niche (see next section and Chapter 4).

In fact, you may be pressed to find a niche without at least one entrepreneur trying to derive a business from it through a Web site. If, for example, you thought that the 10 percent of the population that is left-handed might be a promising niche reachable via the Web, the owners of <www.left-handed.com> thought so too and acted on it before you did. Perhaps a directory of hotels that are friendly to gay people would make up a unique niche? Sorry, <www.gayhotels.com> got there first. How about services for gifted children? Maybe, but you'll be competing with <www.gifted-children.com>.

Of course, you don't have to be the first or only one to identify and take advantage of a niche. As long as enough business is there for a few competitors to earn an acceptable income, there could be a business to be started. In fact, many niches can be further segmented (for example, how about <www.gayhotelsofeurope.com> or <www.lefthandedmusicians.com>?)

Test It First

All sorts of sophisticated market research methods are used to determine whether a market exists, how much it is likely to grow, and so on. However, in the case of lifestyle and other small businesses, I believe that the best way to research is simply to try to get a few sales. All the expensive research you can buy isn't as good as a handful of orders or a handful of cash from the sales you just made. The research question you need to answer is pretty straightforward; it's based on the marketing method(s) being tested: Will enough people buy your product or service at a price high enough that your business concept seems viable?

Test marketing is discussed in some detail in Chapter 4, so please read that chapter if you haven't already. One idea from that chapter that bears repeating is that the Web offers an ideal testing vehicle for certain types of products and services. Although it may not be helpful for locally oriented services, such as teaching music lessons or math tutoring, it can be great for unusual products that have a national or international marketplace. For example, I have done fairly well offering business valuation services over the Internet. In most instances, I can compile a business valuation from my office whether the company I'm valuing is a block away or a continent away. It is the kind of service that people don't buy regularly, so not many have a regular provider of the service. A lot of people are curious enough about the value of their company that they search the Internet using such terms as *business valuation,* so my site <www.small-business-valuations

.com> gets lot of hits. Only a small fraction of those hits turn to sales, but on a cost-per-sale basis, that Web site can be very cost effective.

Keep in mind that the particular mode of promotion you are using is being tested as much as the product or service itself. It is certainly possible that a product will bomb via one promotional method but succeed very well with another. A new product or service is at a clear testing disadvantage because you won't know whether a negative result is due to the product, the promotional method, the price, or the place or time where it's being offered. With a product that is known to sell well by one marketing method at a particular price, a test can offer a more precise answer. If the only variable being changed is the promotion, a good result means that your promotional method is working, and a bad result means that the promotional method is not a good one for that particular product.

If yours is a new business, then you will have to deal with this unknown of promotional method, even with market testing. However, testing is carried out all the time by even the smallest businesses to refine pricing, marketing methods, and the like. If you're selling software to help high schoolers learn geometry and an investment of $500 in a local newspaper brings you an average of 20 sales, your marketing cost of $25 per sale is an established benchmark by which you can measure other possibilities. If you try direct mail and learn that method brings in 30 sales for $500, or about $17 per sale, it is a more cost-effective method than is newspaper advertising. If, however, it brings in 10 sales ($50 per sale), then it is not so cost effective as the benchmark method of newspaper advertising.

Uncovering the Money-Making Angle

Levi Strauss came to New York in 1847 to join his half brother in his struggling dry goods business. In 1853 he joined thousands of others who were heading to California in hopes of striking it rich in the gold rush. Strauss, however, had no intention of panning for gold. Rather, he reasoned that the throngs of miners who were working in rocky soil for hours a day needed good strong trousers. Using the same material from which ship sails were made, he created tailor-made pants to fill the needs of the miners.

Even if this encapsulated history is not totally accurate, the point is that Strauss found a money-making angle for his skills in a place where others weren't looking. Most dry goods merchants at the time were not making fortunes nor were most of the miners. By looking at the situation from a more creative perspective, Strauss did very well and did so within his usually mundane industry.

My point is that you have to stay on the lookout for money-making components, now often referred to as *business models* in your industry. The traditional way of doing things may not be the most lucrative or efficient way to make money using your skills. The most obvious way may not be best either. In fact, it may take some experimentation to find the angle (all right, the business model) that works for your situation. Whether your business is only in the planning stages or you've been at it for several years, you have to be constantly scanning your environment for market needs that you can fill and preferably are qualified to fill. Money-making possibilities come and go, often with only a narrow window of opportunity.

Perhaps there is an opportunity based on repackaging or repositioning your product or service. And perhaps it involves repackaging or repositioning your skill and offering it to a different market in a different way. A while ago, *The Today Show* had a story about a group of professional race car drivers who set up a business teaching teenagers how to drive—not the basics but rather advanced skills to make them more competent drivers. All parents of licensed teenagers worry about their young drivers' lack of experience in handling emergencies race car drivers have the professional skills to teach them to handle and thereby compensate for the lack of driving experience. It's a win for the teen driver, a win for the worried parents, and, more pertinent to this book, a win for the race car drivers cum entrepreneurs.

Sometimes, a money-making opportunity may be based on your in-place expenses (fixed expenses or overhead). If you rent an office, the rent is the same whether you use it 8 hours a day or 24 hours a day. The same goes for business equipment and just about anything else you own or rent. Our primary income in the video business came from contracted production services; that is, a client would pay us an agreed-on fee to produce a commercial or sales program to the client's specifications. We had a good deal of expensive equipment for which the bank expected a monthly payment whether we used the stuff once or 50 times during that month. Because we seldom had paid production work for every day of each month, we began producing video seminars without an up-front charge to the client. Instead, we would make a deal whereby the client, who was already in the live seminar business, would sell the video seminar along with his or her live seminars, and we would split the revenues. This business model proved to be more lucrative than the more traditional contracted service method.

Examples of finding income-generating methods by repositioning a product or service in some way are endless. It takes some experimentation and some risk, but sometimes those risks pan out and lead to far more lucrative businesses.

Considering Your Competition

Competition is a fact of business life, so don't fall into the novice entrepreneur's trap of thinking there's no competition. No matter how good your product or service is, no matter how unique, you have competition. In some instances (rare ones at that), competition is only indirect. For example, suppose you are running a summer tennis school for young teenagers and yours is the only tennis school within 100 miles catering to that niche. You're free of direct competition, but you're still competing for customers and their dollars with several other businesses. Families may be thinking about where to send little Jackie this summer, deciding between your tennis school, a soccer school, an arts and crafts camp, and a sleep-away camp, meaning you are competing with two camps and a soccer program despite the fact that their offerings are very different from yours.

Learning about your competition is covered in more detail in Chapter 4, but several points merit inclusion in this section.

How Will You Compete?

Much of what I've said so far involves the concept of market niches. I even go so far as to say that finding and mastering an appropriate niche is at the core of small business success. Indeed, it is the concept of the market niche that allows very small businesses to compete successfully. A tiny retailer could never successfully compete with Wal-Mart if they chose to do so head on—in terms of price, selection, and promotion. However, thousands of specialty retailers compete quite successfully with Wal-Mart (and other mega retailers) by specializing in a tiny market segment and serving that segment better than the big guys can. Take just about any product as an example. The local Wal-Mart undoubtedly sells more children's clothing in a day than the tiny cotton clothing company in my neighborhood that is open only three days a week sells in a year. Yet that little part-time business can succeed and make money in that niche because it services it in a way that Wal-Mart isn't equipped to and probably isn't interested in serving.

Small businesses compete by positioning their product or service to a clearly defined niche and keeping focused on that niche. To do this, you must understand your niche. Suppose you are a tennis pro who wants to start a lifestyle business teaching tennis. You do your research and learn that the underserved niche in your area is children between the ages of 8 and 11. If you have expertise, or at least some experience, in teaching that age group, positioning yourself to capture that niche may be a great idea. If all your teaching experience, however, is with adults, this may not be the niche for you despite its need for servicing.

Mastering a niche may give you a fighting chance against competitors, but it doesn't guarantee immunity. In fact, seeing someone successfully service a market niche is the greatest incentive to others to enter that niche. So even if competition is sparse now, it may not be sparse forever.

To compete successfully within a niche, a *distinctive competency,* or *distinctive advantage,* can help. Staying with the tennis instructor example, a distinctive competency might be a reputation in tennis as a superinstructor. If you can advertise that you trained two Olympic medalists, you clearly have an advantage over the competition (especially that niche within a niche that has high-level tennis aspirations for their kids).

If you can't make a claim to Olympic-level prodigies, you may have other distinctive advantages. Suppose you are a local part-time middle school gym teacher known to many prospective customers in your target market. Your day job gives you a clear advantage over someone else without the same access to prospects that you enjoy.

Barriers to entry as a control over competition. *Barriers to entry* is a business term that simply means obstacles for new competition. As discussed in Chapter 4, they can be a great benefit or a frustrating impediment depending on which side of the barriers you find yourself.

If you're trying to break into a niche, you must analyze the barriers to entry and honestly evaluate whether you can efficiently break through these barriers. Once you're established in a market niche, barriers to entry are seen in a positive light. From the inside looking out, barriers do a great deal to keep your business up by limiting the competition. The ideal, of course, is to get into a situation where *you* can pass through the barriers but few others can.

Of the many types of barriers to entry, some of the more common (several of which were previously noted) are

- Distinctive competencies
- Money
- Professional licenses
- Specialized knowledge
- Proprietary products or process

Distinctive competencies. Distinctive competencies, as explained previously, are advantages that give a company a competitive advantage. In other words, distinctive competencies of companies that have them serve as deterrents to competition—barriers to entry. As a lifestyle entrepreneur, you should avoid industries with significant barriers to entry, unless you are on the right side of those barriers.

Money. This is the classic barrier to entry. Many businesses, such as overnight delivery services, oil refining, computer chip making, and automobile manufacturing are pretty much closed to small business, largely because the start-up is so costly that money is an insurmountable barrier to entry. In fact, this is one of the important plusses for a large company in deciding on an industry to enter. If money is not a barrier to entry, if entrepreneurs can enter an industry with limited capital and compete on relatively equal footing, big business management will take a skeptical view of that industry. Conversely, few lifestyle entrepreneurs have the capital or inclination to enter businesses that require large up-front investments.

Professional licenses. Several professional groups, ranging from physicians to real estate brokers to hair dressers, must be licensed by the state in which they want to practice their profession. The more publicized rationale for requiring licenses is to assure a level of competence on the part of those who are treating your illness, selling your house, coiffing your hair, or providing a host of other services. Another result of requiring licenses is to control the number of people practicing in that profession and thereby controlling the amount of competition.

Some licenses, of course, are harder to get than others. To attract capable people who are willing to go through years of medical school, internships, and rigorous exams, for example, there has to be a promise of rewards at the end. The promise for physicians in training is the likelihood of a high income (as well as prestige), and to guarantee that high income, the number of practitioners must be tightly controlled.

Professional licenses are a clear and obvious barrier to entry. If you don't have that license to practice medicine, architecture, or dentistry, you are simply barred from working in those professions. If you have a license that few others are able to get, you have the security of knowing that the amount of competition you have will be controlled by the state licensing authorities (and other barriers to entry).

Specialized knowledge, skill, or talent. By no means do all fields require state licensure. Some professions, including many that demand highly specialized skill and knowledge, don't require, or even offer, licensing. Neither computer programmers, nor college professors, nor many types of engineers receive licenses to practice their profession.

Specialized knowledge alone provides a barrier to entry. At this writing, several types of computer programming skills are in high demand. In some cases, the salaries being offered are astoundingly high, and traditional requirements such as college degrees are frequently waived. Despite the promises of high salaries and other perks, many positions go unfilled simply because there aren't enough people who have, or who are in a position to develop, the requisite programming skills.

Professional athletes are not licensed, and the salaries some are paid make the most highly paid programmers (or doctors or lawyers or just about anyone else for that matter) seem like paupers. The prestige of a professional baseball or football player is arguably higher than that of a governor or senator (two other professions that don't require licensure). This wouldn't occur unless the barriers to entry were very high, which indeed they are. That barrier is talent, and only a miniscule proportion of our population has the talent to attempt professional sports.

Proprietary product or process. The U.S. government, as well as other world governments, grant patents as a way of economically protecting inventors. Patents, of course, form a barrier to competition, though seldom a completely insurmountable one because patents are purposely so specific that determined new entrants can often develop functionally similar products if not exact duplicates. Sometimes proprietary (secret) processes, though not patented, form a competitive advantage and therefore a barrier to effective entry, if they are really better than readily available processes.

For example, a friend of mine is in the real estate revaluation business. His company seeks contracts with towns that periodically revaluate all the privately owned real estate in that town for tax purposes. Although several competitors can compete for the contracts, my friend has proprietary revaluation software that in the eyes of the town decision makers is better than that used by his competitors and thus gives him a clear competitive advantage, serving as a barrier to entry to new competition. If you have a better way of making a product or providing a service that can't be easily copied, you may have a barrier to entry on which you can capitalize.

Using The Four *P*s Of Marketing to Compete

The four *P*s of marketing discussed earlier in this chapter are the basic tools that you can work with to compete for customers. Here is an overview of how these tools can be used.

- *Price.* You must consider your prices in relation to those of your competitors. This doesn't necessarily mean you have to match or beat their prices. If your product or service is differentiated in some way (for example, perhaps it is highly specialized or perhaps perceived as better), a higher price can often be justified in the mind of the consumer. In fact, sometimes a higher price will be perceived as indicating higher quality (the reason why "you get what you pay for" is a popular cliché). If something is priced too far below the competition without a clear reason, it becomes suspect as of lower quality or flawed in some other way.
- *Promotion.* Your target market needs to know you are there. Other things being equal, the company with more and better promotion will get more business. Managers of larger businesses think in terms of more money equaling better promotion. Money helps, but a lot of smaller companies can use creativity to compensate for tight budgets.
- *Place.* Perhaps you can offer an advantage to your customers in terms of convenience. If, for example, you are one of four tennis pros offering lessons to young teens, but you are closest to the town's middle school, you have the advantage of convenience.
- *Product or service.* Surprisingly (or perhaps not), established companies tend to fall down in this area. That is, a product or service must be regularly adjusted and improved to meet the changing needs of customers. Established companies with successful products tend to resist change, making them susceptible to eager new competitors ready to embrace

change and gear their offerings to meet the needs of the target market. Designing your product or service to better meet the needs of your target market can be a significant competitive advantage.

Summary

Early in this chapter, I quoted from a marketing text a definition of marketing as *those activities that relate an organization successfully to its environment.* Marketing is at the heart of a business. A company of any size must successfully relate to its environment to survive, so if marketing does indeed relate a company to its environment, its importance can't be overstated.

The traditional tools to do that involve the famous four *P*s of marketing: product, price, promotion, and place. There are infinite ways to use these tools by themselves and in combination with one another. Deciding how best to use them and combine them is the challenge that will make or break a business.

Adding to the complexity is the reality of free market competition. There is always competition, though sometimes it is only indirect. Many entrepreneurs claim otherwise, but they are fooling themselves.

Lifestyle businesses, in fact most smaller businesses, need to find a niche that they can effectively service, preferably in ways that few others can match. Mastering a niche is the most effective way to beat the competition and ultimately have a successful small business.

CHAPTER

6

Financing Your Venture

In an ideal business, income comes in before expenses come due. In reality, very few businesses are so fortunate as to avoid start-up expenses that precede income. It could easily take several months before income meets, let alone exceeds, expenses. In fact, even most established businesses often have at least occasional cash needs that current income can't cover.

This chapter deals with anticipating cash needs and meeting those needs, even in periods when business income doesn't meet expenses. Chapter 9 deals with basic strategies for managing money to wring the most out of every dollar that comes in and for saving on taxes by using the arcane business tax laws to your advantage, no matter how small your business may be.

Estimating Your Revenue and Expenses

Before launching your business, and before figuring out how you'll finance your new business, you need to estimate your start-up and monthly operating costs and your projected monthly revenue. This seems obvious, but you'd be surprised at the number of new entrepreneurs who never take this essential step. Many entrepreneurs take the view that "what will be will be, and I'll deal with cash problems and other problems as they come up." Others reason that accurately projecting expenses, and especially projecting revenue, is impossible, so it's not worth bothering with.

It's true that accurately projecting revenue for a new business is often impossible. It's not quite as difficult to project expenses, but accuracy is still a challenge. However, it's not so impossible to test for reasonableness. That is, if you've done a modest amount of research as suggested in the previous chapter, you should be able to make some reasonable guesses about expenses and revenue, at least to the extent that you can decide whether your concept has merit as a business. For a relatively straightforward business, projecting expenses is no harder than sitting down and listing your initial (start-up) expenses and your recurring monthly expenses. You will have to look up or otherwise inquire about rates and prices for the services and supplies you'll need. Add at least 20 percent to your estimates for possible omissions and other unexpected costs.

Projecting revenue is harder but doable within a reasonable range. Say you followed my previous advice and spent four days trying to get orders for your product. Suppose you secured three orders of $350 each and that each unit you sell costs you $50 ($50 cost per unit). It is reasonable to project perhaps three to five orders per week based on that test, resulting in net sales (after unit costs) of about $5,000 per month. It is stretching reasonableness to anticipate sales of $7,500 per month and clearly not reasonable to anticipate sales of $10,000 per month (at least not in the early stages).

It is often a good idea to base sales projections on three assumptions: lower-than-expected sales, expected or most likely sales level, and better-than-expected sales. In the example of three orders at $300 (net of your cost per unit) over four days, monthly sales projections might look like this:

Monthly Sales Projections

	Lower Than Expected	Expected	Better Than Expected
Unit sales	8	16	20
Dollar volume (net)	2,400	4,800	6,000

Of course, revenue is only part of the story. Let's use the middle column, the most likely sales outcome, as our basis for projection. Let's assume that projected monthly expenses for the mythical business are $1,200.

Monthly gross revenue	$ 4,800
Monthly expenses	1,200
Monthly (pretax) income (monthly gross revenue minus monthly expenses)	3,600
Annual pretax income ($3,600 × 12) =	$43,200

Based on the assumptions made, we'd have a good indication of a go decision, assuming the owner would be happy with an income at this point in the range of $43,000 per year. If the projected expenses were a bit higher, say $1,600 to $1,800, then we'd be in a proceed-with-caution zone; and much higher than that, we're entering deeper and deeper into the danger zone.

You should at least calculate the monthly revenue you need to break even and be convinced that you can get to breakeven soon (as in before your money runs out) and get beyond breakeven—it's hoped well beyond it in the not-too-distant future.

Breakeven Analysis

Different entrepreneurs have different financial goals when they start a business. But it's fair to say no entrepreneur starts a business to lose money. Although there are lots of mathematical formulations for calculating profit and loss under different scenarios, I'll only outline the most basic here: breakeven analysis.

Because breakeven depends on fixed costs and because most fixed costs are paid monthly, breakeven is generally calculated on a monthly basis. Most lifestyle businesses are services businesses, which makes the breakeven calculation very easy. Let's use a piano teacher as an example. The piano teacher would have to know three things to calculate her monthly breakeven point:

1. *Her monthly fixed cost* (expenses that are the same each month such as rent, telephone, Internet service provider, etc.). For this example, we'll assume monthly fixed costs of $200.
2. *Her average revenue per lesson.* For this example, we'll assume her normal charge is $24, but a few students get discounts, making her average collected revenue per lesson $22.
3. *Her average costs per lesson* (also known as *variable costs*). The teacher visits students in their home, so she has automobile expenses for each lesson. Also, a few students pay by credit card, so she must pay the credit card company about 3 percent for each lesson paid for with plastic. Her average costs for each lesson is $2 (variable cost), so her average revenue per lesson, net of expenses per lesson (unit cost) is $20. This $20 goes toward her fixed expenses until they are paid, and the rest, once fixed costs are paid, is income to her.

The formula for breakeven is: Fixed costs / (unit revenue – unit cost). So in this example: Breakeven = 200 / (22 – 2) = 200 / 20 = 10.

To breakeven the teacher must complete ten lessons per month. With modern computerized spreadsheets, it's easy to create a table to show breakeven as well as profit and loss based on the number of units sold (in this case, lessons):

Fixed cost	$200
Average revenue per lesson	22
Average cost per lesson	2

Number of Lessons per month	Collected Revenues	Total Unit Costs	Profit or Loss
1	22	2	($180)
2	44	4	(160)
3	66	6	(140)
4	88	8	(120)
5	110	10	(100)
6	132	12	(80)
7	154	14	(60)
8	176	16	(40)
9	198	18	(20)
10	**220**	**20**	**0**
11	242	22	20
12	264	24	40
13	286	26	60
14	308	28	80
15	330	30	100
16	352	32	120
17	374	34	140
18	396	36	160
19	418	38	180
20	440	40	200
21	462	42	220
22	484	44	240
23	506	46	260
24	528	48	280
25	550	50	300
30	660	60	400
35	770	70	500
40	880	80	600

Another way to view breakeven and profit or loss at different sales volume is with a simple graph, sometimes called a *profitgraph* as shown below for our mythical piano teacher. The upward sloping line indicates her monthly income, based on the number of lessons completed and the price charged. The amount earned after monthly overhead expense (at $20 per lesson after variable costs) is shown on the vertical axis. The sloping line starts at the –$200 mark (the piano teacher's monthly fixed costs). If she gave zero lessons in a given month, she would lose $200 for that month. The point where the sloping line meets the horizontal line (ten lessons) is her breakeven point. Any point above the horizontal line represents profit, and points below the line represent loss.

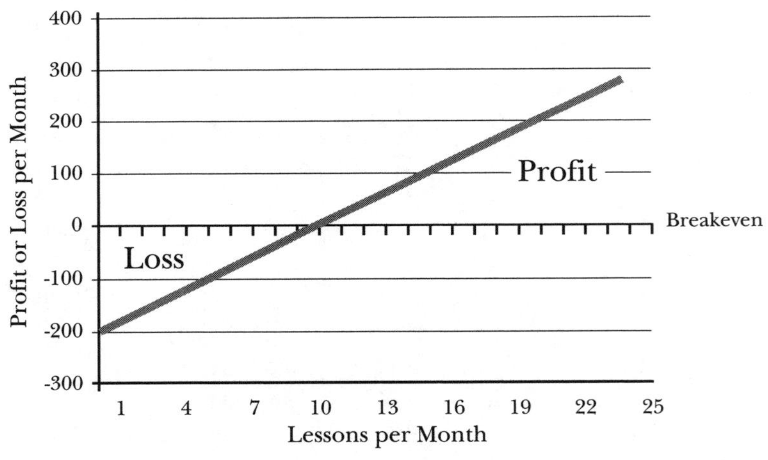

If you are selling a product rather than providing a service, the principles are the same, but your unit costs are likely to be higher. If you're making and selling underbed storage bins, for example, unit costs would include wood, nails, delivery, and so forth; and unit revenue would be the amount you collect for each unit you sell minus your costs for each unit.

Breakeven analysis can get a lot more involved than this. It is used not only to find the breakeven point but to estimate profit and loss using several different assumptions for units sold, pricing, changes in cost structure, and so on. Most lifestyle entrepreneurs don't need these complexities in their own analysis, but it is important to get a handle on how much you have to sell and at what price to break even. It is also important to see what your earnings are likely to be at various reasonably estimated sales levels. Breakeven analysis is an excellent, and sometimes sobering, tool to test the reasonableness of your contemplated venture.

Again, this seems like an obvious exercise. It is not unusual when I create a simple spreadsheet with a client's income and expense projections and show the client that the business can't work based on his projections. The usual reaction: change the projections to meet the desired outcome. Business reality just doesn't respond to this kind of wishful thinking.

I once had a social worker as a client, who saw an opportunity that at first glance looked quite promising. Nursing home residents in his area needed the kind of therapy he could provide. In fact, the need was so huge that he figured he could easily hire three additional social workers and keep them busy almost full-time. What's more, Medicare and Medicaid would pay for these services. My client could provide the services without charge to the recipient and send the bill to the world's most creditworthy payer: the U.S. government.

However, when I asked a few more questions and entered the information into a spreadsheet on my computer, the venture didn't look quite so promising. First, the government's reimbursement rates were fixed. My client would ostensibly come out ahead on each hour of service after paying the social worker who provided that service but not by a lot. When I asked how long it normally took to get paid by Medicaid and Medicare, the concept lost even more of its appeal. Typically, according to him, payment would take 90 to 120 days. His social worker employees would have to be paid perhaps 5 to 10 days after providing services, meaning he would have to borrow against the money owed by the government. Add interest costs. Further, Medicare and Medicaid could be reasonably expected to disallow—governmentspeak for refuse to pay—about 5 percent of the claims. Whether the government paid or not, my client was responsible for paying his employees and his other expenses such as rent, transportation, billing, and secretarial.

By accepting all of his numbers without any modification by me and comparing his projected income with his projected expenses, the bright prospects for his venture dimmed. The company would be operating at a small loss if everything went according to projection. It would be operating at a large loss if the income projections were too high, if the cost estimates were too low, or if any expenses were overlooked.

He was incredulous and insisted on changing the projections to make them work.

This, of course, was doable but not without tossing reasonableness out the window. Despite the fact that people were in need of these services and the government would pay for them, this business was destined to lose money.

I wish I could say he eventually saw the mathematical logic, but I can't. He insisted that this business would make lots of money given the marketplace need. He spent the dollars and efforts to start it and, sure enough, had to close it a year later at a significant loss, a loss in line with the projections based on his own estimates of income and expenses.

The lesson here is to make your projections honestly. You have to accept the numbers, even if they differ from what you want them to be. Wishful thinking and gut feelings have to take second place to financial realities.

The Cash Budget

A cash budget (or *cash flow projection statement*) is a tool, invariably produced today with a computer spreadsheet, that helps in pinpointing cash positions for a business into the short-term and medium-term future. It is developed simply by estimating income and expenses, usually on a monthly basis, and simply subtracting the latter from the former. Cash budgets are discussed in detail and demonstrated in Chapter 8 (see the section in that chapter titled "The Business Plan Constructor").

A highly recommended book for more information on preparing financial projections is *Anatomy of a Business Plan* by Linda Pinson (Dearborn Trade, 2001).

Financing: What Are the Possibilities?

Financing in this context refers to the cash needs for starting and running a business. Most businesses need initial money to get started before they can generate income, and many have periodic cash shortfalls—times when the income generated falls short of the expenses incurred. Start-up expenses can be as small as a phone line and stationery or as substantial as a fleet of airplanes.

Most books on small business discuss financing in terms of venture capital versus debt financing with possible mention of nonprofessional investors, such as wealthy relatives and friends. The majority of lifestyle businesses rely on financing from their owner's own resources (like savings accounts), from their owner's credit cards, and from home equity–type loans for which the owner accepts repayment responsibility. Although personal loans, such as credit card or home equity lines of credit, are not designed for financing business ventures, they often are put to that use. Even though bankers may frown on the practice, they seldom prohibit it outright, tending instead to look the other way at this fairly common practice.

Financing by Using Your Own Resources and Consumer Credit

I think that lifestyle companies, whenever possible, should be funded without using traditional business-financing vehicles. Self-funding is probably cheaper and definitely easier to obtain than outside funding; what's more, it keeps you more independent, which is so essential to most lifestyle entrepreneurs. Typically, self-funding takes the form of financing from the owner's cash resources, using personal credit channels to borrow, or borrowing from friends and relatives. Following are discussions of these major possibilities for self-funding and funding based on your own nonbusiness credit resources.

Home equity loans. If your cash needs at start-up are beyond your available cash resources, a home equity loan is worth considering. This, of course, assumes that you own a home that has some equity value. If you have access to this type of credit, using it would be far easier and cheaper than a formal business loan would be. Your home would be collateral for the loan, but that would likely be the case with a small business start-up loan as well.

If you are considering leaving a job to go into business, apply for a home equity line of credit before you actually resign. Banks are more comfortable lending to someone who is employed than to someone who leaves a job to start a business. Be careful about signing anything that prohibits you from using the loan proceeds for a business venture, but banks seldom place that kind of restriction on a home equity loan. In fact, much of bank marketing for home equity lines of credit stress how you can use the money for any purpose that you please.

Credit cards and other unsecured personal credit. Credit cards and other forms of consumer borrowing are convenient and easy to be sure, but they are also expensive. For small amounts of money, especially if you believe you can repay the loan relatively quickly, I think this route is worth considering, but I would not advise using high interest credit card loans for more than a few thousand dollars. The rates are so high that the interest expense can threaten the prospects of an otherwise viable small business if used to excess.

Friends and relatives. For some this can be a sticky area, whereas for others it is an easy way to get the necessary money to get started. I can't comment on the personal dynamics of seeking financing from friends and relatives, because there are as many variations on those dynamics as there are, well, friends and relatives. Suffice it to say that this can be a ready source of financing and may also be your only viable option. Many businesses are no doubt started thanks in large part to the financial assistance of friends and relatives.

I do advise that the terms of the financing be clearly defined up front. Is it an investment or is it a loan (the difference is explained later in this section)? In either case, what are the specific terms of the arrangement? I can't give advice on the relationship dynamics, but I can say from experience that people often get into misunderstandings because of different up-front assumptions. You don't want to have to someday say, "What do you mean pay you back? That money was an investment that unfortunately didn't work out for either of us." Nor do you want to hear: "Hey, I don't want to be paid back just principal and a few dollars of interest. That was an investment in the company. I want a share of the profits!"

Be clear at the outset what you're asking for and what you're offering. It can save a lot of personal grief later.

Outside Financing

If you intend to seek more formal business financing, such as a business loan or venture capital, you will need a business plan (see Chapter 8), a document that details your plans for your business and your financing needs. The plan explains the marketplace rationale for your venture and the methods you plan to employ to exploit the market need demonstrated in the plan. It also details your projected income and projected cash needs at the outset as well as along the way, usually on a monthly basis.

A plan does not by any means guarantee you'll get the financing you're after. It is a prerequisite to just being considered for financing. Even though business plans for new businesses tend to be quite involved and elaborately packaged, they don't have to be. If you're seeking outside financing (or even if you're not), read about business plans in Chapter 8.

Lending versus Investing

For the needs of most lifestyle companies and, in fact, for most small companies in general, there are two basic types of outside financing: debt financing (lending) and equity financing (investing). In reality, even though these are indeed the basic forms of business financing, they can be used with myriad variations in a multitude of combinations. Therefore, a great variety of financing options are available, though all but the basics are beyond the scope of this book. The two basic forms of outside financing are defined in the sections below.

Debt Financing (or Lending)

Debt financing simply means that a person or organization lends money to another person or an entity like a corporation. Compensation for the loan is interest; that is, the borrower pays the money back to the lender at an agreed date or by an agreed-on periodic schedule with an agreed rate of interest. If your business borrows $1,000 for one year at an agreed rate of 10 percent, at the end of that year the business would owe $1,100 (the $1,000 principal amount plus the interest of 10 percent of that amount).

The calculation gets trickier if payments are made periodically (usually monthly), because the principal is lowered with each payment, but the concept remains the same.

A basic principle of finance is that the greater the risk, the greater the potential reward. Or conversely, the lower the potential reward, the lower the risk that is justified. Interest rates, and in fact the decision to accept or reject a loan on the part of the lender, is based largely on the perceived risk the lender is accepting. Small business, especially start-up small business, is perceived as high risk by lenders, so rates are considerably higher than they would be for, say, Microsoft or Wal-Mart, or even for an established small company.

Remember, because all that lenders are entitled to in compensation is principal plus interest, they can't be expected to take large risks—there is no potential large reward no matter how well the company does. In the case of banks lending to small companies, adequate collateral is usually demanded as a condition of making the loan; a bank wants to know there is some security, something of value, that it can take away and sell if the loan it makes can't be paid by the borrower. Stocks and bonds can be used as security as can a house or other real estate. Understandably, entrepreneurs are reluctant to offer their house as collateral for a business loan. Equally understandably, banks are reluctant to make loans to entrepreneurs without a house or some other form of collateral as security, just in case.

As a practical matter, banks generally won't make a loan unless they think it can be paid back without requiring such drastic steps as foreclosing on someone's house. Despite their image as uncaring, banks don't want to take away a borrower's residence except as a last resort. Even if a borrower has difficulty meeting the loan terms, most banks try to restructure the loan (e.g, stretch out payment terms) to avoid this drastic step. But if the amount of money is significant enough and if the bank believes it has no other reasonable options for collecting the money owed it, it can and will take away a house or any other asset used as collateral in obtaining the loan in order to be repaid the money owed.

A businessperson doesn't have to offer his or her house as security on a loan nor does the bank have to make the loan without adequate security. In most instances, small business loans do include a personal guarantee by the owner, in essence stating that if the business can't pay, the owner will take personal responsibility for repayment of the loan. Exceptions to personal guarantees are most likely in cases of businesses that own tangible assets with enough value that the bank can use those assets as adequate collateral to cover the amount being borrowed.

Small Business Administration (SBA). Because small businesses, especially start-ups, have difficulty getting bank loans, the federal government established the Small Business Administration (SBA) to make borrowing a little more accessible to entrepreneurs. Through its direct lending programs and guarantee programs, it makes borrowing possible for entrepreneurs who are not quite acceptable as risks to banks. Most of its lending activities involve guarantees to banks; that is, the SBA will promise a bank that if a guaranteed loan isn't repaid by the borrower, then the U.S. government, through the SBA, will repay most of the money owed on the guaranteed loan. Of course, the SBA has strict criteria for writing guarantees and, typical of a government agency, a lot of paperwork.

Under the guarantee program, you must start with a bank, be turned down, and then seek the SBA guarantee. Practically speaking, most banks involved with small business lending are familiar with the SBA's guarantee policies and will bring up the possibility with a prospective borrower if appropriate. In fact, some banks can actually write loans based on SBA specifications and automatically obtain the guarantee as long as proper criteria and rules are followed by the bank.

The SBA does have some *direct lending programs,* whereby it lends money directly to small businesses. The direct lending programs change periodically as does the amount of funding available for the programs. A current program that could be helpful to lifestyle entrepreneurs is called the MicroLoan Program. According to the SBA, here's how it works:

> The MicroLoan Program provides very small loans to start-up, newly established, or growing small business concerns. Under this program, SBA makes funds available to nonprofit community based lenders (intermediaries) which, in turn, make loans to eligible borrowers in amounts up to a maximum of $35,000. The average loan size is about $10,500. Applications are submitted to the local intermediary and all credit decisions are made on the local level. (<www.sba.gov/financing/frmicro.html>)

Under this program, the community-based lenders set their own collateral requirements and must offer basic business training to their SBA borrowers.

There are currently direct lending programs available for disabled persons and veterans, but at this writing neither program has funds available for direct lending, a situation that changes periodically. Note that veterans are entitled to a degree of *special consideration* under the bank guarantee programs. Such special consideration, according to the SBA, includes:

- Liaison personnel in each field office;
- In-depth management counseling and training assistance; and,
- Prompt and priority processing of any loan application. (<www.sba.gov/financing/frvets.html>)

Even though the SBA guarantee program has been around in more or less the same form for many years, the direct lending and other programs tend to change. It is worth periodic checks of the SBA's Web site <www.sba.gov>. Also periodically check your local office because it will know, for example, if a certain program is about to receive funds for local lending as well as what the local lending climate is at any given time. You can find your local SBA office on the SBA's Web site at <www.sba.gov/regions/states.html>.

Besides money-lending activities, the SBA provides published materials, seminar programs, and other aids to small business at no cost or minimal cost. By all means, take a look at its site and download any and all material that might be helpful to you in getting started.

Lending and the Lifestyle Business

Lenders' primary concern is getting paid back with interest and according to the agreed payment schedule. A lender theoretically shouldn't care whether you intend to work 12 hours a day, 7 days a week or 1 hour a day, 3 days a week. In the real world, though, lenders are not overly sympathetic to prospective borrowers who are starting businesses for lifestyle reasons. When talking to prospective lenders, I wouldn't stress the lifestyle aspects of your venture. Rather, stress the soundness of your concept and the unwavering stability of your cash flow—especially that portion of it that will be earmarked for making your loan payment on time every month.

Equity Financing

Investing (for purposes of this book and for most lifestyle businesses) literally means buying a portion of a company. When someone buys a stock in a company like Ford or Wal-Mart, that person is buying a tiny piece of that company. If there are 5 million shares of stock issued for ABC Co. and you own five shares, you own one one-millionth of ABC Co.

Suppose your newly incorporated company we'll call XYZ issues 1,000 shares of stock (in most states, you can form a corporation with any number of shares you like, regardless of the company's size, although in some states you may have to pay additional fees if you issue more than a set number of shares). Your company has $10,000 in a company checking account (put there by you), owns no other tangible assets, and owes no money to anyone. Suppose further that you approach me to ask if I might be willing to invest in your private (not public) company. I look over your business plan, we discuss the plan, and I'm suitably impressed. I offer to invest $5,000 for a 30 percent interest in the company. If you agree to this, I write a check for $5,000 to XYZ, and the company gives me 300 of the 1,000 shares. I now own 30 percent of XYZ. If the company goes bankrupt, I lose my investment with no recourse. If the company becomes the next Microsoft, and I retain my shares, I own 30 percent of a multi-billion-dollar company.

My risk here is high—many small companies fail, and only a fraction go on to become large companies. Even if the company succeeds, and even though I own 30 percent of it, there is no ready market for my shares to be sold as there would be for a public company. Although a lender takes a small risk and expects only a small return (payback of the loan plus interest), a small company investor takes a large risk in the hope of a large return on that investment.

For the kinds of situations to which this book is addressed, this simple example illustrates equity investing. Note that there are restrictions on soliciting buyers for shares of stock in your company. It is seldom a problem to invite a few friends, family members, or business associates to invest. What isn't okay is to offer shares to too many people or to do so publicly. States set their own definitions for "too many people" and "publicly," and so does the federal Securities and Exchange Commission. If you're doing more than inviting a few people who you personally know to invest, it is best to clear your offering with your lawyer.

Another warning: In most states you can *authorize* more shares than are actually issued. For example, you may authorize

2,000 shares but initially issue only 1,000. Recalling the example above, I bought 300 of your company's 1,000 issued shares and thereby became the proud owner of 30 percent of your company. Now if the company did well and you decided to issue the remaining shares of the company to someone else, it would lower (dilute) my ownership percentage to 15 percent and make me very unhappy. This is why there are restrictions against issuing authorized shares to the detriment of shareholders. Again, check with your lawyer before issuing shares previously authorized. In fact, if you have unissued but authorized shares, check with your lawyer before selling any of the shares.

Equity Investing and the Lifestyle Business

Equity investments in lifestyle businesses are rare except from friends and family. Investors are looking for a solid potential reward for themselves in proportion to the significant risk they are taking. They are decidedly less interested in your goal of having more family time or pursuing your passion for antique restoration. Further, investors in small companies want to see a clear path for *cashing out,* or getting their investment out with whatever profit that investment has earned. This typically takes the form of either selling the company and dividing the proceeds among the equity holders or offering stock to the public in an initial public offering (IPO). If you are starting your company for lifestyle reasons, neither selling your company nor going public is likely to be in line with your goals.

Equity investors in most lifestyle businesses are those who are involved in the business on a day-to-day basis, not outside investors interested primarily in financial return on their investment. In the unlikely event that your lifestyle business is an exception to that statement, following are sources of outside investments in small business.

Venture Capital

Venture capitalists and venture capital companies are in the business of making equity investments in private companies. Many, if not most, of today's household names of high-technology and Internet companies either started with venture capital or were able to grow rapidly through venture capital investment that came into the company after start-up.

Ostensibly, venture capitalists make their investment decisions based on a company's business plan and on researching the market and competition in that company's industry. In actuality, venture capital people base a large part of their decisions about where to invest on the management of the companies being considered. An entrepreneur with a business plan judged only so-so by a venture company but with three past start-ups that went public would have an easier time getting a new venture financed than would an entrepreneur with a wonderful plan but no track record.

Venture capitalists are professional investors. Sometimes they use their own money, and sometimes they use money invested by people and companies they have assembled to put together a venture fund for the purpose of making venture investments.

The nature of the venture industry is to accept high risk in the hope of high return. A typical venture company may see 40 percent of its investments fail entirely, another 40 percent succeed marginally, and 20 percent do well enough to carry the failures and the marginal successes. Further, different venture capitalists have different policies, but most are only interested in making investments of at least a few million dollars. This may sound strange to a lifestyle entrepreneur who needs $20,000 to get started, but it is logical from the venture capitalist's perspective. Even a fairly large venture company may invest in only five or ten deals a year. Venture companies do a good deal of up-front market and other research on each investment that is being seriously considered. Such research can easily cost $50,000 or more, making even an attractive investment of a few hundred thousand dollars less attractive, because the overhead in research expense waters down the potential return on that investment.

Although an investor in a venerable, publicly traded company like General Electric may be satisfied with a return on investment (ROI) of 8 percent or 9 percent a year based on the perceived risk involved, an investor in smaller, less stable but substantial public companies may expect 14 or 15 percent growth as a minimum ROI. A venture capitalist, who is assuming a much larger risk, may expect an ROI in the area of 30 or 35 percent a year. The bottom line is that unless you can convince a professional venture capitalist that your venture will produce that kind of return (and your persuasion holds up to empirical research and scrutiny), you have little chance of obtaining formal venture capital.

Angels

Angels are like informal venture capitalists—individuals who made a good deal of money (probably in business) and now make occasional venture capital investments. You won't find them listed in the Yellow Pages or advertised anywhere else, partly because investing isn't their main line of business but mostly because they don't want to hear from every aspiring entrepreneur out there with a business plan.

Angels often make investments of a few hundred thousand dollars (rather than in the millions as professional venture companies do). Further, they typically like to make investments in industries they know about and feel positive about. An angel who made his millions through an early e-commerce company would be more likely to invest in an Internet company than in a company that imports raw materials.

Even though most lifestyle businesses would not be attractive investment candidates for most angels, such investments are not out of the question. Your best chance for this type of funding would be to find an angel investor who knows your industry and has a soft spot for it. A nice thing about angels is that they like to be involved in the companies in which they're invested, at least in an advising capacity. Their advice should be most welcome given their likely track record of success in the industry in which they've succeeded.

Finding angels. As I've said, angels don't make themselves easy to find. You might ask your lawyer or CPA or other business associates. Organizations exist that act as clearing houses for angels, seeking business plans from entrepreneurs and sharing them with angels who might be interested. They generally don't reveal the name of the angel to the entrepreneur. When angels get a plan that interests them, they contact the entrepreneur to discuss the possibility of an investment.

One such clearinghouse is called JMI Venture Capital Network, which can be found on the Web at <garnet.acns.fsu.edu/~jostery/venture.htm>. Also, the Web site <www.capital-connection.com/networksangels.html> provides information on angel financing and has links to additional angel clearinghouse sites.

Summary

Most lifestyle entrepreneurs are best served by financing their ventures via their own resources. If your resources are inadequate, borrowing through a personal vehicle such as a home equity loan is a viable option, or even credit card lines of credit can be used for small amounts of money (less than $5,000, for example). Depending on the relationship dynamics, relatives and friends may be a reasonable source of financing. Formal business loans, too, are a possibility for the lifestyle entrepreneur, but they require a business plan (see Chapter 8) and probably adequate collateral, including a personal guarantee. Outside investment from venture capitalists or angels can be considered but are seldom appropriate for, or available to, the lifestyle entrepreneur.

CHAPTER

7

Legal Structure

Every business, even if its owner thinks of it merely as a hobby or a source of a few dollars of extra income, has a specific legal structure that is either purposefully chosen or chosen by default. In the case of many small businesses, the default choice—sole proprietorship—may be fine, at least in the early stages. The structure, whether chosen by the business owner or by default, can have a significant impact on taxes, on the owner's responsibility for unforeseen legal problems, and even on whether the owner can be held responsible for unpaid debts if the business runs into serious difficulty.

Many new entrepreneurs are convinced that the first thing they need to do is incorporate. Somehow, the popular opinion seems to be that only a corporation can be a *real* business. Incorporating is essential in some cases, but in many small business situations it isn't necessary or even helpful. This chapter outlines the most popular forms of legal structures for small business and some of the pros and cons of each. It is always a good idea to check with your attorney before settling on a legal structure.

Corporations

A corporation can be thought of as an artificial person created to conduct business. Legally, it is in essence an entity that is separate from its owner or owners. A whole body of laws and ever-changing tax regulations apply specifically to corporations but not to real people directly.

Advantages

One of the major advantages of corporations is that they minimize the liability (legal responsibility) of the owner(s) of the corporation. For example, suppose you're a computer network expert who forms a corporation called Up and Running Network, Inc., and you fund it by placing $2,000 in its checking account on January 1. The corporation has no other cash, owns no other assets, and owes nothing to anyone. Suppose that on January 2 you get a call from someone who wants you to integrate the computers in his company's offices. You write up an estimate on Up and Running Network, Inc., stationery that say's your company will do this job for $1,500. The customer signs the estimate form and you start the job.

Suppose you inadvertently drop a tool inside the client's main server. The company's owner sees this, claims you destroyed his server and lots of data, and sues you for $100,000. He really won't be suing you because he's doing business with Up and Running Network, Inc., so his legal recourse is to sue Up and Running Network, Inc. Now Up and Running has assets worth a total of $2,000 (the amount you put in its checking account). This fact alone would likely discourage him from suing, as the litigation would cost more than $2,000. If he does sue and wins a judgment of $100,000 (or any amount of $2,000 or more), all he'll get is $2,000 because the corporation, not its owner, is responsible–and $2,000 is all the corporation has. The corporation would go bankrupt and its assets (the $2,000) would be given to the business owner (or the company) that sued it. For practical purposes, that would be the end of the story from a legal perspective. You could elect to then start up a new corporation after suffering a lot of unpleasantries to be sure but a financial loss of only $2,000. Had the same thing happened but you were working as yourself (a sole proprietorship), you could have been responsible for the entire amount for which you were being sued. If you owned a house and the suing business owner prevailed in his suit, you could have lost your house if you had no other assets available to pay the $100,000.

This example is overly simplified, but it does illustrate the basic point that responsibility for a corporation's obligations and liabilities are with that corporation and not with its owner(s). There are, however, exceptions to this principle. The Internal Revenue Service, for example, can hold owners responsible for taxes (and penalties) due. In some rare circumstances, such as fraud or deception, the court can *pierce the corporate veil,* allowing owners to be held responsible for a corporation's liabilities. Also, professionals practicing in some fields can't get around liability for malpractice by hiding behind a corporation; they must carry insurance to avoid potentially devastating financial judgments for malpractice.

The same protection applies to money the corporation owes for any reason; a corporation's owners aren't personally responsible for its debts. Even if the worst happens and a corporation goes bankrupt, its owners don't take on the corporation's liabilities. Again, there are certain exceptions such as in cases of fraud and deception. Also, banks and other creditors are keenly aware of this protection from liability so they often require owners of small corporations to agree to personally guarantee the corporate debts owed them. In other words, if you *personally guarantee* an obligation of a corporation, you will be held responsible if that corporation doesn't pay.

Another key advantage to incorporating is the ease of transferring and sharing ownership. When a corporation is formed, it is divided into small segments of ownership called shares of stock that are issued to the owners (shareholders). Staying with the Up and Running Network, Inc., example, let's say 1,000 shares were issued when the corporation was formed. Each share then equals 1/1,000 of the total company ownership. If I own all 1,000 shares, I of course own the company. I can at any point decide to sell some or all of my shares. If I want to take in an equal partner, I can sell 500 shares to her for whatever price we agree on, and now we each own half of the company. If the two of us decide we want to take in one more or ten more partners, all we do is sell the new partner or partners (more accurately, the new shareholders) the appropriate number of shares.

Dividing up a proprietorship is far more difficult. In fact, usually the best strategy for taking in a partner in a proprietorship is to first incorporate, as discussed in the partnership section below.

Disadvantages

Corporations come with a few disadvantages that are explained in the following sections.

Separate taxation. A corporation is considered a separate entity from its owners. As such, it is also taxed separately (more accurately, in addition to) its owners. Profits of the corporation are taxed separately from the salary the owner or owners earn from the corporation and even from profits the owner(s) receive from the corporation. For example, suppose I am the owner of Up and Running Network, Inc. The company earns enough to pay me a salary of $40,000 and still have a profit of $20,000. I personally pay taxes on my salary, and the company pays the employer portion of my Social Security tax and Medicare taxes. In addition, Up and Running Network, Inc., must pay taxes on the $20,000 profit. If and when I take the after-tax portion of the

$20,000 profit out of the corporation to give to myself, I must also pay taxes on the amount I receive personally.

As a practical matter, there are ways to get around a good deal of this double taxation. For example, if I'm the sole owner, I can merely raise my salary to $60,000 or pay myself a bonus of $20,000, thereby eliminating the profit and the taxes associated with it. However, I must do this before the end of the company's tax year, and of course that money would be fully taxable as income to me. If I'm on the calendar year (as most lifestyle businesses are), I can pay myself a bonus on December 31, but I can't do so on January 1 and have it accounted for in the previous year.

Another solution is to elect to be an S corporation, which is a corporation in every legal sense, except it isn't subject to the double taxation because the profits automatically *flow through* to the owner(s). S corporations are discussed in more detail below.

Cost to establish and maintain. There are expenses in setting up and maintaining a corporation. For a small company, these costs are proportionally quite steep. Legal fees can easily be $500 to $1,200 to set up a corporation. States charge anywhere from $100 to several hundred dollars for the initial filing and then charge again for every year the corporation is maintained.

Many states assess other fees, such as annual filing fees, to maintain a corporation. To a large or even medium-sized corporation, these fees may be trivial. To a lifestyle or part-time business, they can border on prohibitive.

Paperwork. Corporations require many forms to be filled out and filed—tax forms, annual reports, and other forms that government agencies periodically require of corporations. Needless to say, filing delinquencies and omissions result in fines and penalties by government authorities.

S Corporations

An S corporation (as opposed to the more common type of corporation described above, which is technically a C corporation) is a corporate structure designed for smaller businesses. It is a corporation in every legal sense, except that it isn't subject to the double taxation to which other corporations are subject. All profits of an S corporation automatically *flow through* to the owner(s), who must pay taxes on them based on their own tax situation, just as they would from profits received from any other corporation. However, the S corporation itself doesn't pay corporate income taxes to the IRS. Note that if an S corporation has losses, those losses, too, flow through to the shareholders and can generally be subtracted from shareholders' other income to reduce their tax liability.

Certain restrictions apply, but they shouldn't be an issue to most lifestyle businesses nor other very small businesses. An S corporation can't have more than 75 owners, can't be owned in whole or in part by another corporation(s) that isn't also an S corporation, and can't be owned in whole or in part by anyone who isn't a U.S. citizen or legal resident. If you decide that incorporation is the way to go, be sure to check with your lawyer and CPA about the possibility of an S corporation.

A good book about setting up and taking full advantage of the S corporation structure is *How to Form Your Own "S" Corporation* by Ted Nichols and Robert Friedman (Dearborn, 1999).

Sole Proprietorship

This is your default structure if you don't choose otherwise. Most lifestyle businesses start as sole proprietorships, and many remain that way for their entire existence. Contrary to popular opinion, a sole proprietorship can be a *real* business and can be very profitable.

Some sole proprietors do eventually decide to incorporate. There is no prohibition against incorporating a sole proprietorship at any point.

Advantages

The prime advantage of being a sole proprietorship (often just called proprietorship) is simplicity. You merely start doing business. There are no forms to fill out to become a proprietorship and no forms to maintain a proprietorship structure. Taxes on income from a proprietorship are accounted for on your regular tax return by using an additional schedule called a *Schedule C.*

Disadvantages

The disadvantages of a sole proprietorship are an exact reflection of the advantages of setting up as a corporation. That is, you have no layer of protection against legal responsibility for anything the business does. Legally, you are the business and the business is you. If the business is sued, it means you are sued. If the business owes money, you owe money.

Also, transfer of ownership, particularly partial transfer of ownership (such as taking on a partner or partners) is a bit more difficult. As a practical matter, many proprietorships decide that the easiest way to solve the mechanics of taking on a partner is to incorporate in preparation of that event.

Though a proprietorship is fine for most lifestyle businesses, at least in the early stages, exceptions do exist. The most likely exceptions would be situations with major risks of liabilities. A business, no matter how small, that is engaged in teaching parachute jumping, alligator wrestling, or even horseback riding, for example, should probably take advantage of the legal protections offered by the corporate structure.

Partnership

In its everyday usage, a partnership means two or more people owning a business together. In actuality, many businesses termed partnerships in day-to-day conversation are actually corporations or other legal entities. In a true partnership, each partner has the right to fully represent the partnership. This means any one of the partners can write checks, enter into contracts, and otherwise make decisions that legally bind the partnership.

A partnership doesn't have the separate legal entity status that a corporation does and therefore doesn't have that extra layer of protection from legal responsibility. In fact, any of the partners in a true partnership can be held liable for the actions of the partnership. If the partnership is successfully sued as a result of the actions of one partner, the winner of that suit can pursue any of the partners personally to collect the judgment.

A partnership doesn't pay taxes on its profits. Instead, the income flows to the owners, who pay taxes based on their own tax situation. Neither partnership ownership nor partnership income has to be spread evenly among the partners. For example, if Person A owns 90 percent of the partnership and Person B owns 10 percent, than 90 percent of the profits would flow to Person A and the other 10 percent to Person B.

If you are planning a business together with another person or persons, be very careful about setting up a casual partnership. Legal advice is essential. A lawyer would probably advise setting up a corporation as the legal entity. Otherwise, the lawyer would probably advise that a clear and formal partnership agreement be worked out between the partners that specifically covers responsibilities, ownership, transfer of ownership (taking in a new partner or selling the entire partnership), and more. The corporate structure would, in all likelihood, be cheaper to set up than would writing a suitable partnership agreement. It would have the added advantage of the layer of protections against liability and a ready-made method for transferring ownership (by selling shares of stock).

Limited Liability Companies (LLCs)

Limited liability companies, or LLCs, are a relatively new form of business organization designed specifically for smaller businesses. In some ways, LLCs have the advantages of a sole proprietorship and a corporation without too many of the disadvantages. Though they are new legal structures that are not as well tested or established as corporations, proprietorships, or partnerships, they are well worth looking into for lifestyle companies.

In their short history, they have been used primarily for companies that have more than one owner (proper terminology for LLC owner is *member*), but they may well be just as appropriate for single-person companies. As of this writing, all states except Massachusetts and the District of Columbia allow single-member LLCs.

Advantages

LLCs offer the same protection from liability that corporations offer. Except in extraordinary circumstances, members are not personally responsible for debts or potential lawsuits of the LLC.

LLCs are taxed (or more accurately not taxed) like S corporations–that is, the tax consequences flow through to the members–but LLCs provide more flexibility in this area than do corporations. Profits of a corporation flow through to the owners based directly on their proportion of ownership. If I own 20 percent of XYZ, Inc., and XYZ has a profit of $10,000, then 20 percent of that profit ($2,000) must flow through to me, as must the tax consequences of that profit. In the case of LLCs, though, flowthrough doesn't necessarily have to be in direct proportion to ownership. Members can adjust the proportions within IRS guidelines such that members receive different flow-through proportions from their ownership proportions.

For example, suppose Bill and Mark set up a company. By agreement, Bill puts up the $10,000 needed to start the company, and Mark puts up most of the work time needed to get the company going. If the company is an LLC, they can easily decide on a 50-50 percent split of the profits (or any other reasonable proportion), despite the disparity in the capital invested. Though they could set up a corporation and divide ownership to achieve the same division, that is more cumbersome and expensive. Suppose further that they also decide that the 50-50 percent split is fair for the first two years, but after that Mark should get 65 percent of the profits. With an LLC, this is as easy as agreeing to it. With a corporation, it get much trickier to achieve this change in division of income.

As with S corporations, losses, too, and the tax benefits created by those losses flow through to owners (members) and are accounted for on those owners' personal tax returns. Unlike with S corporations, the losses and the tax benefits accompanying those losses can be allocated by the LLC members; they don't have to be in proportion to the ownership interest of the members.

Finally, LLCs may be easier and cheaper to set up than are corporations, especially in the case of a one-member LLC; and they can be set up without a lawyer. Generally, you must prepare and file LLC Articles of Organization with your state's LLC filing office (typically the corporations division of the secretary of state's office). A few states require the publication in a local newspaper of a simple notice of intention to form an LLC prior to filing your articles. Usually, the filing including the LLC's Articles of Organization is a matter of filling out a fill-in-the-blanks form.

Disadvantages

Selling an LLC or taking in a new partner can be a bit more difficult than it would be with a corporation. Transferring full or partial ownership in a corporation can be as simple as selling shares, whereas ownership interests in an LLC cannot be readily transferred. In general, to transfer ownership current members of an LLC have to agree to a transfer of a membership interest unless the transfer involves only the right to receive profits or the return of capital invested in the LLC. In the case of a one-member LLC wishing to take on a partner or partners, a whole new entity has to be formed.

Another issue, at least at this writing, has to do with the self-employment tax, which is essentially Social Security and Medicare taxes paid by self-employed people. The first $84,900 (as of late 2002) of most people's earnings is subject to a Social Security tax of currently 12.4 percent, and most people's entire earnings are subject to a Medicare tax of 2.9 percent. Employees who are not self-employed pay half of these taxes in the form of a payroll deduction, and their employers pay the other half. Self-employed people pay close to the same amounts through the self-employment tax. However, nonwage and salary earnings, such as profits from a corporation (dividends), are not subject to this tax. Owners of small privately held corporations can and do allocate their earnings between salary and profit with an eye toward the tax consequences. In most instances, profits from an LLC are subject to self-employment taxes, even if they are not allocated as salary.

As a rather new organizational structure, the LLC—and its implications—is not fully understood by businesspeople, accountants, and lawyers. In fact, rules and policies are still evolving, and those rules and policies differ from state to state. This uncertainty in and of itself can be something of a disadvantage as it is difficult for lawyers and accountants (and authors) to give definitive advice. On balance, however, the LLC structure is worthy of serious consideration for many small business and lifestyle entrepreneurs. For good protection against legal liability without the up-front expense and complexity of a corporation, this may be the ticket.

Current LLC information. Because LLCs are new and evolving and because the rules governing them differ from state to state, it is important to get current and state-specific information before choosing this structure. A helpful Web site for LLCs (and other small business legal information) is <www.nolo.com>. For state-specific information, call the secretary of state's office in your state and ask for the department that handles issues regarding corporations.

Professional Services Corporations

In most states, certain professionals—generally those that need state licenses to practice, such as accountants, physicians, dentists, lawyers, psychologists, and social workers—who wish to incorporate must do so as professional corporations (PCs).

Professional corporations are protected against most forms of liability by the corporate shield just as other corporations are. The important difference is that professional corporations are not protected against malpractice liability, which is the reason states force professionals into this special corporate structure. Practicing professionals who don't want to assume personal liability for malpractice (which includes virtually anyone with any sense) must purchase malpractice insurance. If this weren't the case, a doctor might order the amputation of a patient's healthy right arm, leaving untouched the diseased, left one, be sued for malpractice, and walk away from liability by hiding behind the corporate structure. The professional corporation concept is a welcome method of protecting all of us from such egregious malpractice.

A professional services corporation can elect S corporation or C corporation status, but all shareholders must be practitioners of the profession for which the corporation is formed. The sole purpose of a PC must be to render the services of that profession. Although most corporations can legally enter a variety of businesses, a dental PC, for example, can't decide to also start a used car lot or even a toothpaste factory. Nothing prohibits the same dentists from starting a new (non-PC) corporation to sell used cars, make toothpaste, or become involved in another industry.

If you are a licensed professional or have any question whether your status may be covered by this restriction, call your secretary of state's office (probably the corporations department) to find out if your profession is one that is required to incorporate as a professional services corporation.

Legal Structures and Health Insurance

Health insurance is a major issue for many new (and established) entrepreneurs. Many people thinking about leaving a job to start a business are held back by fears about insurance coverage, discussed in more detail in Chapter 14.

Until 2003, most business entities, other than C corporations, could deduct only a portion of the expenses for health insurance for their owners. However, as of 2003, owners' health insurance is generally 100 percent deductible for all business entities. There are certain restrictions, such as, for example, the deduction for health insurance can't exceed an owner's salary (or owner's or partner's income), except in the case of C corporations, where health insurance deductions can exceed such salary or income.

Before 2003, the choice of legal structure had a significant impact on the deductibility of health insurance expenses for many lifestyle entrepreneurs. Several people who would have otherwise chosen alternative structures set up C corporations simply to utilize the more generous health insurance deductibility. Now the C corporation advantage is very much mitigated by the new and more extensive deductibility rules for other types of business entities.

Heath insurance and the self-employed and lifestyle entrepreneur are covered in Chapter 14.

CHAPTER

8

The Business Plan

Virtually all small business advice books insist that the fledgling entrepreneur start with a business plan. Advisors to entrepreneurs also exhort their advisees to prepare a comprehensive business plan. Books are written on the subject, and college-level courses teach the preparation of a business plan.

A plan can be useful to the start-up business, and in some cases it can be absolutely essential. I will say nonetheless that many successful businesses have started without any business plan at all, and many more have started with a very simple plan, numbering only a few pages in length. Still more small businesses do prepare plans but only to satisfy the requirements of investors or lenders.

The preparation of a simple plan can be quite helpful. It needn't be 80 pages long nor does it have to be printed on expensive cotton weave paper. But reducing your business concept and direction to writing can help you clarify and think them through as well as find flaws and even solutions to those flaws. Moreover, a business plan is an excellent way to communicate your concept and your intended method of carrying out that concept to others, such as lenders, investors, and advisors. It can even be used to gather opinions from others that could help you to improve your concept and its implementation.

Think of a basic business plan as a road map of where you're going, the route you'll take to get there, and the reasons why. Above all, accept the fact that the plan, no matter how comprehensive or how great, will never be good enough to be followed religiously. Modification of the plan and variance from the stated direction will most certainly be necessary.

For the purposes of both this book and most lifestyle businesses, I discuss only the very basics of a business plan. If your planned business is complex or if you intend to seek venture or investor capital, you'll need more than this section offers. A few recommended books on the subject are:

- *Anatomy of a Business Plan,* by Linda Pinson (Dearborn Trade, 2001)
- *The Business Planning Guide: Creating a Plan for Success in Your Own Business,* by David H. Bangs (Dearborn Trade, 1998)

The basic components needed for a business plan are outlined below. Following the component outline is a *business plan constructor,* which allows you to build a business plan by answering several questions in writing. Finally, the chapter includes a sample business plan based on the business plan constructor.

Components of the Lifestyle Business Plan

The most essential components of a business plan include the following:

- *Concept.* Explain your overall business concept in a paragraph or two. Include the kind of business you plan to start, the reasons it is needed, and the target market it will serve. Don't hesitate to include a sentence about how this will be a part-time or lifestyle business if that is indeed the case.

- *Research steps.* Outline the research steps you have taken to date that indicate that the business concept is viable. If you haven't taken those steps yet (see Chapter 4), explain the steps you will take. If you haven't taken any research steps nor intend to explain briefly why you are sure your concept will succeed.

- *Financial projections.* Projecting your income and expenses is an important part of your plan, granted such projections can't be done with great accuracy, especially the income projections. However, they can be done accurately enough to estimate the reasonableness of success. For more information on projecting income and expenses, see Chapter 6 and read through the section on the "Cash Budget" later in this chapter.

- *Financing.* Detail the financing requirements your business has in terms of its start-up and its day-to-day operations. This section should be written in conjunction with, and using information from, the financial projection section. Detail whether the needed cash will come from investors, lenders, your own resources, or a combination of several sources. Of course, this section has to be much more comprehensive if you are seeking outside financing than if you are financing your business with your own cash resources. Financing and obtaining financing is discussed in Chapter 6.

- *Marketing.* Explain the marketing rationale for your concept and your method of marketing. Note that marketing does not mean only advertising and promotion but includes an analysis of your defined target market, competition, and pricing, as well as getting the word to prospective customers and persuading them to become actual customers. Marketing is discussed in detail in Chapter 5.

- *Legal structure.* A business may be a sole proprietorship, partnership, corporation, limited liability company, or some variation thereof. Your intended structure should be spelled out, even if spelling out merely means declaring "the company will be a sole proprietorship for the time being" (the default structure automatically imposed if no other structure is specifically created). The pros and cons of incorporating and other legal structure issues are discussed in Chapter 7.

The Business Plan Constructor

This section contains an easy-to-follow outline that can be used to construct a business plan. Although this outline may not produce a plan adequate for major venture capital funding, it should suffice for most lifestyle businesses. Even in the case of entrepreneurs with aspirations of larger enterprises that involve major venture financing, this outline should be an excellent first step toward the kind of comprehensive plan that venture investors expect.

To follow the business plan constructor, fill in each section as indicated. Respond to the phrases and answer the questions as indicated. The phrases in parentheses and bold italics are suggested section headings. A paragraph or two will suffice for most sections, but feel free to answer in as much detail as you need. The idea is to help you think through your business and your plans, and organize your thoughts by reducing them to writing.

Some sections, as indicated, are designed for the needs of such outside financing sources as bankers, investors, friends, or relatives. You may omit these sections if you aren't planning to finance your business with outside funding (that is, if you are financing it with your own available resources).

Following this business plan constructor is a sample business plan created by using this constructor.

B U S I N E S S P L A N

Business Plan Constructor

BUSINESS SUMMARY

Briefly summarize your business concept. Summarize the products and/or services you plan to offer and to whom you plan to offer them (your target market).

If you're already in business, outline your company's history to date, including past successes and difficulties and current opportunities.

This section is meant to be a summary of what is to come. Limit your description to a paragraph or two. Elucidating details will be included in later sections as indicated.

INDICATIONS OF VIABILITY

Summarize the research you've done and the reasons that indicate this business concept has a good chance of succeeding.

Note: Read Chapter 4 for details on pre-start-up research.

The purpose of this section is to demonstrate to yourself and others that objective indications exist that your concept is a viable one. This includes:

- An indication that there are no legal prohibitions against doing what you are planning to do (if you've consulted a lawyer and received a green light, this can be as simple as stating that "According to Attorney John Jones, whom I consulted, there are no legal obstacles to operating this type of business").
- An indication that a market truly exists that needs or wants your product or service.
- An indication that you can profitably gain access to that market (no insurmountable barriers to entry).

BREAKEVEN

Calculate the point at which you will break even on a monthly basis.

Note: See the section regarding breakeven calculations in Chapter 6.

It is important to estimate the level of sales you need to at least break even on a monthly basis. As detailed in Chapter 6, this is a matter of estimating your monthly fixed expenses and your gross profit margin. If you wish, you can add a breakeven table or graph to illustrate projected profit and loss and breakeven point (also detailed in Chapter 6).

GOALS AND OBJECTIVES OF THIS VENTURE

Summarize your goals. Virtually all business plans include a section on goals and objectives that often takes on a different character in the case of a lifestyle business. In the traditional business plan, the objective is always growth in some form(s). Traditional goals (goals being defined as concrete milestones toward the objective) may be to increase average sales amounts, to increase market share, to gain a cost and price advantage to undercut competition, and so on.

Although the plan for the lifestyle business may certainly include goals relating to increased sales, growth, and competitive strategy, it may also include lifestyle goals. After all, for lifestyle entrepreneurs, lifestyle goals are the whole reason for going into business in the first place.

For this section, outline your business goals and your concept for growth. For any business that is just starting up, of course, growth has to be part of the plan. Define the scope of your growth goal. "I want to grow" is not an adequately expressed goal. Define your goal in a discreet and measurable way, such as "I plan to grow to the level of $100,000 per year gross sales by next year and $150,000, the following year." It may be a good idea to delineate your business goals in a timeline: first-year goals, second-year goals, and so on.

Add your lifestyle objectives as well in this section (or in a separate section, if you prefer). Though few other small business authors would approve, I think it's important to include such goals as these:

- "I want to limit working hours to four days per week."
- "This business will be designed to allow me to make a specific contribution to the public (or specific segment of the public) while providing me with a reasonable income."
- "The primary objective of this business is to allow me to spend after-school hours with my two children while providing me with an income."

I approve of defining lifestyle objectives in your business plan, but I do advise that you remove that section if you present the plan to outsiders in order to attract financing. Bankers and others in a position to provide small business financing much prefer that your goals are traditional business goals and that your waking hours are fully dedicated to the money-making aspects of your business.

PROCEDURES

Outline your methods and procedures. If the service you're offering is not immediately self-explanatory, explain how you will run the business. If, for example, you're teaching piano in your home, and you've stated that in the Business Summary section, then you can skip this section. However, if your proposed business is based on unusual or not readily understood procedures, a bit of explanation is in order.

If, for example, you are offering clients an innovative method to back up computer files, you need to explain how you will achieve that. Or if you're importing products for sale in the United States, you have to explain how you'll acquire those products, how you'll ship them, and so on.

SUMMARY OF FINANCIAL NEEDS

How much money will it take to start this business? To complete this section, you first need to use the cash flow projection worksheet at the end of this business plan. The worksheet allows you to plug in the estimated income and expenses that will be entailed both before you start your company and during its first year of operation.

This section takes the information from your cash flow projection worksheet and states your financial needs in summary form.

You might start this section with a statement such as "I estimate that this business will require $6,450 to start. In addition, it will need another $1,000 over the first year of operation until positive stable cash flow can be achieved. Here are the major expenses that will be entailed."

List the major expenses involved up front. Using the piano teaching example, list your estimated expenses like this:

Business equipment	$3,000
Inventory for resale	250
Other expenses (recurring and nonrecurring)*	3,250
Total up-front cash needed	6,500
Covering cash flow shortfall through 12 months	1,000
Total including start-up and estimated cash flow shortfall	$7,500

If you are seeking outside financing, prospective lenders and investors will want to see how you're spending your money (or, perhaps more accurately, their money). Even if you are self-financing your venture, it is important to think through your up-front cash needs; and projecting and listing your expenses forces you to do that.

*Expenses such as telephone service, advertising, and the like are recurring expenses (typically monthly). Here, however, we are concerned with such expenses that are incurred before actual start-up. Recurring expenses will be dealt with later. So if, for example your business telephone service costs $30 per month, and you expect to have it set up for one month before you actually start doing business, pre-start-up telephone service expense would be $30.

Once again, this section is designed as a summary of financial needs; the details are delineated later in the section covering cash flow projections. The later section uses a spreadsheet to calculate cash needs on a monthly basis. Create your cash flow projection statement first (explained in detail at the end of this Business Plan Constructor section). Then filling in the summary section will be easy.

FINANCING

How will your business be financed? This section details where you plan to get the needed money.

Summarize your plan for financing. For example:

- I seek $7,500 in funds borrowed from a bank, or
- I seek $5,000 from bank borrowing and intend to finance the balance of needed funds ($2,500) through my own cash resources, or
- I need to borrow $5,000 from friends and family and can finance the balance ($2,500) through my own cash resources.

Note: If you are self-financing your venture, use this section to state exactly where the money will come from. For example, "I will finance this venture with money that I'll withdraw from my savings account at XYZ Bank," or "I will sell the stock I have in ABC Company to self-finance this venture."

MANAGEMENT

Who will manage this business? Merely state who will manage this business. (This business will be managed by __________.)

Management Qualifications

What are the qualifications of the manager(s) stated above to run this company? Entrepreneurs typically think that investors and lenders evaluate a business proposal on the basis of the strength of the idea. In actuality, the strength and qualifications of management are more important criteria in making lending and investing decisions.

Provide details about the background and accomplishments of yourself (and others who will be working with you in managing the company, if there are others). Include education, previous business and management experience, and the like. Concentrate on those background elements that indicate that you (and others, if applicable) are capable of running the business as it is proposed.

A current résumé can be added as an appendix.

LEGAL STRUCTURE

State the legal structure that you have chosen for your business and the reasons for that choice. You don't need elaborate or lengthy justifications. For example, you merely need to say something like "I have chosen to incorporate this business to protect against unforeseen liability" or "To maintain simplicity, this business will be operated as a proprietorship while it is a part-time venture."

If the business will be a proprietorship and you are seeking outside funding, some assurances that unforeseen liability is not a major issue would be a good idea. If you've consulted a lawyer who advised that incorporation is unnecessary, you can merely say, "I consulted Attorney Jones, who feels that this business carries no undue liability risk and that incorporation is unnecessary in terms of protecting against liability risk."

For information on legal structure, see Chapter 7.

MARKETING

The next sections are all components of marketing. I suggest you set up your business plan putting them under the large heading *Marketing*. That is, make marketing a bigger bold heading and list subheadings of that category.

Marketing Summary

Summary of four Ps *of marketing (product, price, promotion, place).* Marketing is made up of four basic elements, often termed the four *P*s—product, price, promotion, and place (discussed in detail in Chapter 5). In this summary section, briefly outline how you plan to address the four *P*s. The remainder of the marketing section delineates your marketing strategy and your marketing plans.

If you are using your business plan to obtain outside funding, point out that many of the components of your marketing plan are detailed below; you don't want someone flipping to this section and deciding this is all you have to say about marketing.

Target Market

Who is your target market? Define your target market concisely—the niche group to whom you intend to sell your product or service.

If you intend to teach piano, saying for example, "My target market is people who want to learn to play the piano" isn't focused enough. "My target market is children between the ages of 11 and 14 who aspire to play piano professionally" or "My target market is children between the ages of 8 and 12 whose parents want them to be instructed at home" are more focused definitions of a target market.

Your initial research should have provided you more-than-sufficient indications that your target market does indeed exist; and those indications should be stated in the research section "Indications of Viability" of your business plan.

Competition

Note: To learn how to find information about competition and how to analyze your competition, see Chapter 4.

List your main competitors along with your analysis of their strengths and weaknesses. You can mention how you intend to carve out a niche to successfully compete. For example, if you plan to teach piano and your main competitor teaches only on Tuesday and Thursday and only at her home, you might state here that you'll compete by teaching on other days and at the student's home.

Don't make the mistake of believing that you have no competition. Be honest with yourself about your direct and your indirect competition (those competing for the same customer dollars that you are, even if they are not offering the same product or service that you are).

Competitive Advantages or Distinctive Competencies

It is important to consider, and reduce to writing, your competitive advantages. They could, for example, be location, access to lower price supplies or inventory, or relevant and unique skills.

If, for example, you are skilled at gaining publicity or have a relevant certification that your competitors do not have, make sure that you exploit it to the extent possible.

Competitive Disadvantages

Though few entrepreneurs like to admit it, some competitors may well have advantages that surpass their own.

Consider how well established your competitors are and how good their contacts may be. Perhaps they have better salesmanship abilities, better financing, or other advantages.

Of course you won't know all of your competitors' advantages or disadvantages, but you may know some of them. It's best to admit their strengths as well as their weaknesses and plan how best to exploit their weaknesses and mitigate their strengths.

Differentiation within Niche

How will your business be differentiated from others servicing your niche? A challenge facing every new business is gaining the attention of its target market and convincing those in that market to consider doing business with the new business. Promotion is the tool to gain initial attention (see the section on promotion in Chapter 5). A key job of that initial promotion is to show prospective customers how this new business is different from businesses already servicing that target market. Take the book that you're now reading as an example. It competes with dozens of other small business books, but it is differentiated because it is designed specifically for entrepreneurs who see their business as a means to a chosen lifestyle. Promotion for the book—press releases, ads, and its very title—stress this differentiation.

Your business needn't be a radical departure from everything else out there. Better service, lower prices, and flexible hours can be adequate differentiation in many cases.

In this section explain how your business will be differentiated from competition *in the view of your target market.* Drawing again on the example of the piano teacher for young children, the target market is probably more concerned with the teacher's ability in dealing with small children than the teacher's musical credentials and accolades.

Differentiation Message

In the simplest terms, what is your message? Explain how you will reduce your differentiation to a message that you can easily communicate to your niche. Messages should be concise and easy to understand. For example:

- Same quality, lower price
- Expert piano instruction at your convenience
- Expert piano instruction in your own home
- Full Web site development within 48 hours
- Color caricature while you wait

Getting Message to Target Market

How will you get your message (gain access) to your target market? After you have focused on your niche, differentiated your business as appropriate, and reduced that differentiation to a concise message, you next need to get that message to your target market. (For additional information on gaining access to your target market, see the section within the marketing chapter (Chapter 5) titled "Access to Your Niche").

Explain here the method or methods you will use to gain access to your target market. If your target market is composed of owners of small businesses, perhaps your plan is to purchase a mailing list of small companies in your area and contact them by direct mail. Perhaps you intend to hire students to place flyers under dorm room doors to inform students of your physics tutoring business. Perhaps you plan to recruit special-need high school students by talking to local school guidance counselors.

As with the other sections of your business plan, you have to think through the steps you must take and then reduce those steps to writing. The task here is to figure out and detail exactly how you will get your message to its intended audience.

POTENTIAL PROBLEMS

What can go wrong with this venture? Few small businesses get off the ground without dealing with a slew of problems. Many entrepreneurs, however, including both those with little experience and those who should know better, sweep those problems under the rug. They either don't want to deal with them or are so optimistic that they don't believe problems can get in the way.

If you are seeking outside financing, it is important to *answer the negatives.* Lenders and venture investors are accustomed to overoptimistic entrepreneurs. If you don't find the potential problems—you can be sure they will. If you find them and admit to them, the impact will be less severe because you will have already considered the potential problems and planned your response and solutions to those problems.

Even if you're not seeking outside funding, this section is important. Thinking through and preparing for the pitfalls and problems can only help. To do otherwise is to take more risk than is necessary.

List in this section the most likely potential problems with a sentence or two of explanation. In the next section, you'll point out solutions to the problems and mitigating circumstances that can lessen their severity.

Problem Solutions and/or Mitigating Factors

How will you make sure these problems don't jeopardize your business? For this section, explain what you will do to minimize the impact of the problems outlined above and how you will defend against them.

Also, explain how the extent of the damage can be minimized if the potential problems do become reality.

Once again, your job is to think through this aspect of your business step-by-step and to clarify and concretize it by reducing it to writing.

The rest of your business plan involves detailing your estimated pre-start-up expenses and your estimated expenses and revenues for at least the first 12 months of operation.

Thanks to modern computerized spreadsheets (such as Microsoft Excel), much of the calculating tedium can be done quickly and easily by computer. The expense and income estimates are demonstrated on a spreadsheet, shown later in this business plan constructor.

ESTIMATED START-UP EXPENSES

List your start-up expenses in detail. List all those expenses you expect to incur in starting your business. In fact, make three lists:

1. In the first list, include business equipment that you will use on a long-terms basis to run the business (don't include items you're buying for resale or such consumable items as your office supplies). Include items like furniture, computer equipment, and any special business equipment (not consumable or disposable supplies) you need to offer your services or make your product.
2. In the second list include inventory—the items and supplies you're buying to resell. Inventory includes items you are buying to resell exactly as bought in addition to items you plan to modify in some way or use as components in the products you offer. If, for example, you are making dolls for resale, you would include the cloth, thread, buttons, packaging (if any), and other items that would be used in creating the dolls and be resold as part of the whole product the consumer would ultimately buy. Also include items used in creating the products that are not ultimately part of the product. For example, if you use masking tape to protect certain areas of the doll while painting it, include the masking tape in this category even though it is later discarded.
3. The next list includes your overhead—business expenses that remain constant regardless of sales level and limited here to those you expect to incur before start-up. Items such as rent, advertising, telephone expenses, and Internet provider fees go on this list but only the amounts that will be incurred before start-up.

The section of this business plan constructor called *Summary of Financial Needs* includes an outline of financial needs. This section is essentially one with the details filled in:

For example:

BUSINESS EQUIPMENT:

Computer equipment	$1,800
Piano stools and related furniture	500
Phone & fax (purchase)	400
Books & materials (for own use, not for resale)	300
Total Business Equipment	$3,000

ITEMS FOR RESALE

Music books	$ 150
Sheet music	100
Total Resale Inventory	$ 250

OTHER PRE-START-UP EXPENSES

(Other expenses that will be incurred before start-up; for such recurring expenses as telephone, Internet services, etc., only the pre-start-up portion is included here.)

Stationery and related printing	$ 600
Advertising (brochures, etc.)	700
Insurance (liability, business in home)	300
Legal and accounting fees	600
Telephone service (separate business line)	30
Internet service	20
Piano tuning	200
Miscellaneous	800
Total Other Expenses	$3,250
Needed to cover shortfall in income for first few months	$1,000
Total Pre-Start-Up Cash Needs	$7,500

Estimate your ongoing expenses. Estimate your expenses for the first year on a monthly basis. Some expenses, such as telephone service and rent, are pretty much the same month to month, but others will vary. If you've budgeted $1,000 for advertising for the year, chances are that amount won't be incurred in 12 equal monthly increments. If you know when it will be spent, allocate it to the proper month(s) as appropriate. If you don't know when it will be incurred, allocate this expense and others like it equally over the 12 months of the year.

Estimated Income, First Year

Estimate your income on a monthly basis. As difficult as it is to project expenses, predicting income over the initial 12 months for a new business is even more difficult. Nevertheless, it is important to make the best estimates you can. I recommend that you actually make three income projections:

1. Best-case scenario
2. Worst-case scenario
3. Most likely scenario

In making projections, use the most likely scenario but err on the side of the worst case. It is easier to deal with more cash than expected than it is with less cash than expected.

The primary purposes of creating cash flow projections is to predict the amounts of cash shortfalls and the points when they occur and then to be prepared to deal with them and estimate when and how much money will be available for the owner(s) to take out of the business.

Your Cash Flow Projection

At the right is a sample cash budget (or *cash flow projection*).

The columns and rows where the numbers belong may look daunting, but they are explained in detail on the following pages.

	Pre-start-up	Jan.	Feb.	March	April	May	June	July	Aug.	Sept.	Oct.	Nov.	Dec.
1 **Cash Balance, Start of Month**	$ 0	$ 0	$1,000	$1,000	$1,000	$1,000	$1,000	$1,000	$1,000	$1,000	$1,000	$1,000	$1,000
2 **Cash Inflow:**													
3 cash sales		350	600	700	750	900	800	550	350	750	900	1,000	900
4 collections from credit sales		0	40	60	60	60	60	40	0	0	60	80	80
5 debt in (borrowed funds in)													
6 owner or shareholder contributions (funds in)	6,500	1,000											
7 other funds in													
8 **Total Cash Inflow**	6,500	1,350	640	760	810	960	860	590	350	750	960	1,080	980
9 **Cash Outflow:**													
10 **Expenses** (recurring and nonrecurring):													
11 stationery and related printing	600												
12 advertising (brochures, etc.)	700	100	75	50	0	40	50	0	0	100	0	50	40
13 insurance (liability, business in home)	300												
14 legal and accounting fees	600	50		250	50					50			250
15 telephone service	30	30	30	30	30	30	30	30	30	30	30	30	30
16 Internet service	20	20	20	20	20	20	20	20	20	20	20	20	20
17 piano tuning	200							200					
18 miscellaneous	800	100	130	130	130	100	100	100	100	100	100	100	100
19 inventory (for resale)	250						200						280
20 **Business Equipment** (buy fixed assets)													
21 computer equipment	1,800												
22 piano stools and related furniture	500												
23 phone & fax (purchase)	400												
24 books & materials (for own use, not for resale)	300	50	50		50		50		50		50		50
25 **Total Cash Outflow**	6,500	350	305	480	280	190	450	350	200	300	200	200	770
26 **Net Cash Flow for Month**	0	1,000	335	280	530	770	410	240	150	450	760	880	210
27 **Cash Balance at Start of Month**	0	0	1,000	1,000	1,000	1,000	1,000	1,000	1,000	1,000	1,000	1,000	1,000
28 **Current Cash** (net cash flow + cash balance at start of month)	0	1,000	1,335	1,280	1,530	1,770	1,410	1,240	1,150	1,450	1,760	1,880	1,210
29 **Owner's Draw** (money taken out of business)	0	0	335	280	530	770	410	240	150	450	760	880	210
30 **Cash Balance at End of Month**	0	1,000	1,000	1,000	1,000	1,000	1,000	1,000	1,000	1,000	1,000	1,000	1,000

The overall purpose is simple. It is to calculate and show the following:

- The pre-start-up expenses
- The estimated income for each month
- The estimated expenses for each month
- The amount of cash available at the beginning and end of each month
- The cash shortfalls and when they will occur (if any)
- The projected amounts and points where money can be taken out of the business by the owner

This cash budget is for the pre-start-up period and for the first year of operation. It is a good idea to update and extend your cash budget periodically (perhaps every 3 months) so that you always have a budget going forward for 12 months based on relatively current data.

Immediately following the sample cash flow statement and explanation is a sample business plan that uses the business plan constructor outline. It includes a cash flow projection statement for the hypothetical business proposed in the business plan—that of a jewelry dealer.

Cash Budget: Explanatory Notes

This is a line-by-line explanation of the sample cash budget (cash flow projection) on the previous page. The hypothetical part-time piano teaching business is a sole proprietorship with no employees other than its owner.

1. Cash balance at start of month. The estimated checking account balance at the start of each month. The remainder of the cash budget essentially charts estimated additions and subtractions to and from that checking account. Except for the first column (the pre-start-up period), the amount on this line for each month will be the same as the last line for the previous month (cash balance at end of month).

2. Cash inflows. Section heading indicating that the next several items are additions to the company's cash account (checking account).

3. Cash sales. The estimated total monthly amount of cash sales for this company. Credit card sales can be considered cash sales.

4. Collections from credit sales. The estimated total monthly amount of payments received for credit sales from the previous month(s); although most clients pay for lessons when received, a few clients are billed for their lessons.

5. Debt in. Line for cash inflows from borrowed funds. This company does not plan to borrow money, so no entries are on this line.

6. Owner or shareholder contributions. The owner's own funds that are invested in the business. To prevent a cash shortfall (in other words, to prevent overdrawing a checking account, aka running out of money), the owner adds money from her own funds, both pre-start-up and in the first month of operation. In fact, she prudently keeps her business checking account from falling below $1,000 by adding money if and when necessary (as it is in the first month of operation).

7. Other funds in. All other funds that might come into the business; it is essentially for miscellaneous cash in.

8. Total cash inflow. The sum of all cash projected to flow into the company for each month and for the pre-start-up period; it totals all the lines under the heading of "Cash Inflows" for each month.

9. Cash outflow. Section heading indicating that the next several items are subtractions from the company's cash account (checking account).

10. Expenses (recurring and nonrecurring). A subheading indicating that the next several items are expenses. Three categories of cash outflows are used in this cash budget as defined below:

1. Expenses—goods and services that are purchased and used by the company (not resold) over a relatively short term (less than a year).
2. Inventory—items purchased by the company to be resold in the normal course of business (including finished goods for resale, components, and supplies used directly in making the product to be resold).
3. Business equipment—items purchased and to be used by the company (not purchased for resale) that are expected to last for a long period (more than one year).

11 through 18. Various expense categories that are likely to be recurring items with many recurring on a monthly basis.

19. Inventory. Goods bought to be resold by the company. In the case of the hypothetical company, it is for music books and supplies (reeds, etc.) that will be sold to students.

20. Business equipment. A subheading indicating that all the items to follow are for equipment that will be bought and used by the business over the long term (one year or more). In the case of this hypothetical business, all such equipment will be bought before start-up.

21 through 24. The various items of business equipment that the company will buy in the first year.

25. Total cash outflow. The sum of all cash projected to flow out of the company (all spending) for each month and for the pre-start-up period. It totals all the lines under the heading of "Cash Outflows."

26. Net cash flow for month. The cash flow for each month (and for the pre-start-up period). This line shows the result of "Total Cash Outflow" subtracted from "Total Cash Inflow."

27. Cash balance at start of month. A restatement of line #1 repeated here for convenience.

28. Current cash. The amount of cash projected to be in the business at the end of the month before the owner takes any money from the business. It is the result of adding the "Cash Balance at Start of Month" to "Net Cash Flow for Month."

29. Owner's draw. The amount of money taken out of the business by the owner. Were this business a corporation rather than a sole proprietorship, the owner would be paid a salary and not take a draw. It is highly recommended that a minimum threshold amount be kept in the business's checking account to pay bills, both expected and unexpected. The owner of this hypothetical business has decided to keep a minimum $1,000 in the checking account and take the amount over that minimum as owner's draw. As this is a sole proprietorship, the owner is legally considered self-employed, meaning she is responsible for paying self-employment taxes, income taxes, and possibly other state and local taxes from her business earnings.

30. Cash balance at end of month. The amount of cash in the business's checking account after all inflows and outflows for the month. As noted above, this hypothetical business will keep a minimum of $1,000 in its checking account, and the owner will take the amount over $1,000 as draw at the end of each month.

Sample Business Plan (from Business Plan Constructor)

Now that you have reviewed a template for constructing a basic business plan, let's put it to use.

My friend Sallie imports jewelry from Nepal. I'll use her business as a basis for this business plan. Because the purpose is to demonstrate the construction of a business plan using the business plan constructor, I won't be constrained by the real facts of her business. Instead, I'll take the liberty of changing facts and adding and subtracting elements of her business to better demonstrate the business plan constructor.

ENTREPRENEUR PROFILE

Exporting Jewelry from Nepal

Sallie Fischer grew up in Connecticut. In her thirties, she worked as a manager for a big company in the Midwest. In the summer of 1990, before starting a new job, she decided to take an exotic vacation—a round-the-world trip—which got a lot more exotic than Sallie expected. She fell in love with a Nepali guy, whom she eventually married. They now live happily in Kathmandu with their son (age eight at this writing).

Sallie was always close to her family in Connecticut, which is 9,000 miles from Nepal, and wanted to visit at least once a year. As Kathmandu is hardly a popular destination for American tourists, there are few low airfare deals to and from Nepal, $1,200 per person being about the lowest. And Nepal is not known as the place where you go to become rich; average per capita income is about $250. Though Sallie and her husband were doing fine by Nepali standards, the $3,600 it took for three round-trip tickets was a hefty price.

Nepali craft people make a lot of attractive and unusual jewelry mostly of silver. What's more, this jewelry is very cheap by American standards. Guess how Sallie paid for her annual trips? That's right, she bought a lot of jewelry in Nepal and brought it with her on each visit to the United States, selling it easily to friends, friends of friends, and jewelry and gift shops. Most of the buyers indicated they would like to buy again when Sallie returned the following year. In fact, by the next year, jewelry proceeds were paying the family's airfare. Soon after that, jewelry proceeds were paying for airfare plus a good deal more as Sallie developed a regular clientele.

Sallie figures she can convert jewelry importing into a much bigger and less sporadic business, which some day she might. In fact, she and her husband are strongly considering moving back to the United States to grow her jewelry business.

B U S I N E S S P L A N

Jewelry from Nepal

BUSINESS SUMMARY

This business involves the importing of silver jewelry from Nepal into the United States. During annual buying trips to Nepal, I will purchase jewelry that will be sold both retail and wholesale. Retail sales will be made primarily through jewelry parties that I organize and that a number of other people organize for me. Wholesale sales will be to jewelry and gift shops, primarily in tourist areas in the Northeast. Also, some wholesale sales will be through jewelry parties organized by others.

The marketing section of the business plan includes more details on marketing of the jewelry.

BACKGROUND

I have been living in Nepal for over 12 years but plan to move back to the United States soon. Early in my time in Nepal, I was struck by the quality and beauty of the jewelry made by crafts people there in a centuries-old tradition. Prices are astoundingly low by U.S. standards.

I visited my family in the States at least once each year since living in Nepal, and I paid for these trips (for my husband, my young son, and myself) by buying jewelry here and reselling it in the United States.

As I'll be living in the United States with a young child, I'll need an income as well as time flexibility, because I am the primary caretaker for my son. Also, I still have connections and friends in Nepal whom I want to visit regularly. Importing jewelry seems an ideal way to achieve these goals.

Indications of Viability

My annual visits, financed by jewelry sales, are the best indication of viability that I have. Over the past few years, sales have averaged about $8,000 per year with total expenses of less than $3,500 per year (not including airfare), providing me an income of $4,500 for less than three weeks of full-time work. Further, sales to shops and through jewelry parties have not been unduly difficult.

Since returning to the United States, I have presented samples to nine different jewelry stores in several tourist towns (Mystic, Connecticut; Newport and Block Island, Rhode Island; Stockbridge, Massachusetts; and Rhinebeck, New York). Five of the nine bought jewelry during my unannounced visit. Two others indicated they would buy but currently were overstocked. Only two of the nine said they would not be interested. The average sale was $520.

Though I only visited one or two stores per town, most areas have at least four possible shops that sell this type of merchandise. New York State, of course, has several hundred shops that are potential customers.

BREAKEVEN

Based on my expense projections (see cash budget at the end of this business plan), my monthly overhead will average about $800. This excludes budgeted amounts for inventory purchases because that is a variable, not a fixed, cost. Based on this $800 estimate and on my pricing, which is to at least double my inventory purchase costs, I will need sales of $1,600 to break even each month. This is far less than the average amount I have sold per week during my periodic visits to the United States, so it should not be a problem to achieve this level of sales each month.

Goals and Objectives of This Venture

As stated in the "Background" section of this plan, an important goal is to provide an income while also providing flexibility of my time and periodic travel to Nepal (which will be at least partly deductible as a legitimate business expense).

Specifically, I seek an income of about $25,000 to $30,000 per year from jewelry sales after the first year of operation. Given that sales during my brief annual visits yielded gross revenues of about $8,000, this financial goal should not be difficult to attain. Sales of about $60,000 to $75,000 per year would provide this income.

Summary of Financial Needs

This business will require about $21,000 to start. Pre-start-up expenses are estimated as follows:

Buying trip to Nepal	$3,000
Purchase of initial inventory	10,000
Business equipment	1,500
Expenses (includes initial set-up expenses and contingency for miscellaneous and unforeseen expenses)	6,500
Total up-front cash needed	$21,000

Expenses and income projections for the first 12 months of operation are detailed in the cash budget at the end of this business plan.

FINANCING

I have $24,000 in savings and investments that I can use toward funding this business. I intend to finance the business myself based on my own resources.

MANAGEMENT

I will manage this business myself. In fact, for the foreseeable future, I will be the sole employee of the business.

Management Qualifications

I've been importing jewelry from Nepal and selling it in the United States, albeit on a small scale, for several years. Further, I have relationships with several jewelry crafts people and resellers in Nepal, and I have a working knowledge of the Nepali language. Also, for a couple of years, I worked for an exporting company in Nepal.

LEGAL STRUCTURE

For the time being, this business will be run as a sole proprietorship. My attorney sees no substantial liability risk, and I have no plans to seek outside partners or investors. Further, my accountant, Aaron Michaels, CPA, sees no substantive tax benefits to incorporation for this business, at least initially. However, he thinks the incorporation issue should be revisited at the point where the business starts earning more money, because there may then be tax savings that result from incorporation.

Therefore, I see no reason to go through the expense and paperwork required of setting up a corporation.

MARKETING

Marketing Summary

In essence, I plan to market the jewelry to two groups of resellers: (1) sponsors of impulse-sale parties and (2) jewelry and gift shops in tourist destinations.

Here is the basic summary of my marketing strategy:

- Product—I will sell imported handmade silver jewelry from Nepal.
- Price—In general, I will set prices based on my costs. Specifically, I will sell at a minimum 100 percent markup to resellers and at three times my cost when selling retail (such as at jewelry parties). However, I will adjust prices up or down based on such market conditions as competitor pricing, demand for product, need for immediate cash, and so on.

- Promotion—Most selling to resellers will be by direct sales. That is, I will periodically visit party sponsors and jewelry shops on sales calls, both announced and unannounced. I will also produce a brochure and eventually a Web site. The Web site will be primarily for use by my resellers (to view new products, to reorder, etc.).
- Place—Most marketing will be in New England and eastern New York State. Specifically, I will limit visits to locations that are within four hours by car of New Haven, Connecticut, where I'll be living.

The rest of this sections details my marketing strategy and plan.

Target Market(s)

I am targeting two areas.

1. Women Who Sponsor Selling Parties—There are women who host parties at their homes that include both a social and a business aspect. They demonstrate and sell impulse-buy products and earn a commission on sales. Tupperware (plastic food storage containers) pioneered the concept in the 1970s. I have sold a lot of jewelry through these informal networks and plan to continue targeting this unconventional channel.
2. Jewelry and Gift Shops in Tourist Areas—I have decided to target shops in tourist areas and towns in the Northeast. They are relatively easy for me to approach because there are so many such towns within a day's trip of my home in central Connecticut. More important, I tested this niche, and the test proved quite positive.

Competition

In the Northeast, there is little direct competition for importing jewelry from Nepal. However, I'm really competing with importers from Mexico, India, Bali, and other third world countries, as the country of origin is only one factor for consumers in the buy decision. Although the exotic nature of Nepal helps, consumers care more whether they like the jewelry and whether the price seems reasonable and affordable.

Also, I recognize that I am competing not only with jewelry but with a whole host of gift and impulse-buy items that are sold to and through my target group of sales parties and tourist-town shops.

Buying Plan

I intend to visit Nepal once each year to buy inventory and to maintain my connections there. The bulk of buying and other communications can be done via e-mail and occasionally by telephone. I have already arranged buying procedures through e-mail with several suppliers in Nepal.

Distinctive Competencies

I have contacts in Nepal and knowledge of the country that few direct competitors can match. Speaking the language enables me to go right to the crafts people themselves who generally don't speak English. This means I can get better-quality product and get it cheaper.

If I didn't have these advantages, I don't think that I'd be able to successfully run this business.

Competitive Disadvantages

As stated above, my competition is indirect. I am not worried about others directly importing jewelry from Nepal; rather, my competitors are importing from other countries and selling jewelry and nonjewelry products to the same niche.

Many jewelry importers have better relations with jewelry shops and better knowledge of what those shops want. Also, shop owners know in general how well the products they have been buying for years will sell. My products are a bit more of a risk to shop owners simply because they are untried.

Differentiation within Niche

I will differentiate my product in three ways:

1. Price—It is generally cheaper than jewelry of equivalent quality.
2. Handmade—Consumers like handmade jewelry. The Nepali jewelry that I sell is made by hand, which is relatively rare and becoming even more so.
3. Direct Importer—Shop owners like the romanticism of buying directly from the person who visits the actual crafts people in the country of origin, especially if it is an exotic country like Nepal. They love the stories about the jewelry, the people who make it, and the country itself. Sales-party sponsors and their guests enjoy these stories even more. I always share stories with shop owners and party sponsors—and with party guests when I can.

Differentiation Message

The message is *Handmade Jewelry from Nepal at a Reasonable Price.* The between-the-lines message will stress the exoticism of Nepal, as that is an element of what customers are buying.

Getting Message to Target Market

As most of my selling will be hands-on, getting my message to my target market is easy. I will personally visit sales-party sponsors and jewelry and gift shops in tourist destinations.

I also plan to produce a brochure that will show some of the jewelry in addition to mountains and other scenes of Nepal, as my message includes promoting the exoticism of Nepal.

Potential Problems

Nepal is politically and economically unstable. A significant change or upheaval could have a detrimental effect on this business if it interferes with supply of product or makes export more difficult.

Also, Nepal currently enjoys favorable import status with the U.S. government. Because of its "most favored nation" (MFN) status, handmade silver jewelry is taxed at a very low rate. Changes in Nepal, or in U.S. relations with Nepal, could have an adverse effect on business as my marketing advantage depends in part on price.

Mitigating Factors

Even if there were adverse political change in Nepal, the country will still need foreign trade. Jewelry making is an important component of the country's fragile economy and an embedded aspect of the nation's culture. I believe that any disruptions will be temporary. With my experience and contacts in Nepal, I should be able to secure supplies of jewelry under all but the most adverse set of circumstances.

If the United States increases duties on the kind of jewelry that I import, it will have a negative effect on my profit margins. However, I do have a comfortable profit margin so it would take a very large increase to threaten the business in a major way.

CASH PROJECTIONS (INCOME AND EXPENSES) FOR FIRST 12 MONTHS

I estimate that this business will need approximately $21,000 to start and cover initial cash flow shortfalls. The cash budget on the following pages details my projections for income and expenses for the pre-start-up period and the first 12 months of operation.

Although inventory will not be purchased each month, I am budgeting for periodic inventory purchases by reserving 50 percent of cash received from sales each month in an inventory purchase fund (except for the first month of operation when cash will be tightest and inventory highest). Though I expect inventory costs to be closer to 40 percent of sales based on my pricing, I want to set aside this higher percentage to fund the purchase of a growing inventory in order to accommodate expected sales growth for the first year.

Estimated Income, First Year	Pre-start-up	Jan.	Feb.	March	April	May	June	July	Aug.	Sept.	Oct.	Nov.	Dec.
Cash Balance, Start of Month		$ 180	$1,995	$1,530	$1,525	$1,715	$1,810	$2,140	$2,410	$1,205	$1,900	$1,785	$1,860
Cash Inflow:													
cash sales		1,500	2,500	3,500	3,700	4,000	4,500	4,500	4,800	4,800	5,000	5,300	6,000
collections from credit sales		0	100	500	650	700	750	750	800	800	800	800	800
debt in (borrowed funds in)													
owner or shareholder contributions (funds in)	$20,000	1,000											
other funds in													
Total Cash Inflow	20,000	2,500	2,600	4,000	4,350	4,700	5,250	5,250	5,600	5,600	5,800	6,100	6,800
Cash Outflow:													
Expenses (recurring and nonrecurring):													
utilities (business allocation, home office)	20	30	30	30	30	30	30	30	30	30	30	30	30
telephone (installation, monthly service)	100	25	25	25	25	25	25	25	25	25	25	25	25
Internet service	20	20	20	20	20	20	20	20	20	20	20	20	20
legal and accounting fees	500	150											150
insurance		150											
postage & shipping	60	60	200	150	90	100	100	200	100	250	100	100	120
Advertsing/Marketing:													
sample cases & related brochure & materials	1,900												
produce Web site	800												
host Web site	20	20	20	20	20	20	20	20	20	20	20	20	20
sales calls (travel expenses)		80	140	200	200	200	200	200	200	200	200	170	150
Nepal buy trip	3,000								3,000				
supplies	400		30		40		40		50		60	50	50
miscellaneous	1,500	150	100	60	60	60	60	60	60	60	60	60	80
inventory (for resale)*	10,000	0	1,300	2,000	2,175	2,350	2,625	2,625	2,800	2,800	2,900	3,050	3,400
Business Equipment (buy fixed assets) computer and peripherals	1,500												
Total Cash Outflow	19,820	685	1,865	2,505	2,660	2,805	3,120	3,180	6,305	3,405	3,415	3,525	4,045

*Although inventory will not be purchased each month, I am budgeting for it by putting aside 50% of cash received from the current month's sales into an inventory purchase fund.

Estimated Income, First Year *(continued)*	**Pre-start-up**	**Jan.**	**Feb.**	**March**	**April**	**May**	**June**	**July**	**Aug.**	**Sept.**	**Oct.**	**Nov.**	**Dec.**
Total Cash Inflow	20,000	2,500	2,600	4,000	4,350	4,700	5,250	5,250	5,600	5,600	5,800	6,100	6,800
Total Cash Outflow	19,820	685	1,865	2,505	2,660	2,805	3,120	3,180	6,305	3,405	3,415	3,525	4,045
Net Cash Flow for Month	180	1,815	735	1,495	1,690	1,895	2,130	2,070	(705)	2,195	2,385	2,575	2,755
Cash Balance at Start of Month	0	180	1,995	1,530	1,525	1,715	1,810	2,140	2,410	1,205	1,900	1,785	1,860
Current Cash (net cash flow + cash balance at start of month)	180	1,995	2,730	3,025	3,215	3,610	3,940	4,210	1,705	3,400	4,285	4,360	4,615
Owner's Draw (money taken out of business)	0		1,200	1,500	1,500	1,800	1,800	1,800	500	1,500	2,500	2,500	2,600
Cash Balance at End of Month	180	1,995	1,530	1,525	1,715	1,810	2,140	2,410	1,205	1,900	1,785	1,860	2,015

CHAPTER

9

Managing Money

When he finished his degree in finance, a friend of mine went to work for a large corporation. His job was managing the float on the company's payroll; the company knew from many years' experience the likely percentage of payroll checks that would be cashed and the funds that would be needed to cover those checks one day, two days, three days, and so on after the checks were issued. Most employees cashed their checks within two or three days of their issue, but the company was able to accurately predict the percentage that waited four days, five days, and so on and knew that a small (but predictable) percentage would wait as long as several weeks.

Part of my friend's job was to watch over the payroll account and the flow of checks being cashed. The rest of the job involved making short-term investments with the money that was earmarked for the employee payroll but left temporarily in the company's account. In the rare instances when the statistically based predictions were off the mark, the bank automatically extended credit to the company through a line of credit attached to the payroll account so that no employee check would bounce. The amount of money the company earned from managing the payroll account in this way probably wasn't huge, but it had to be enough to cover my friend's salary and benefits and still leave enough to make it worthwhile for the company to manage the account in this way.

I'm not suggesting that you or someone you hire manage your payroll account this way, but it does illustrate a point about managing money. By diligently keeping watch over the inflow and outflow of cash, you can enhance your earnings and your cash position.

The nature of many businesses is such that far more dollars are often coming in and going out than the owner actually is able to keep. Suppliers, landlords, employees, and others have to be paid; of course, what's left over after everyone is paid belongs to the owner. However, you as the owner also have the ability to increase the amount left over by taking full advantage of the cash that you are stewarding from the time it comes in until the time it goes out. Lifestyle businesses won't be able to find the same windfalls from cash management that large corporations can. But managing cash to maximum advantage is arguably more important for a small business, where cash flow problems can threaten the very existence of the business. Most small business owners can add a few dollars to their pocket through the use of certain basic cash management principles. At the very least, effectively managing your cash flow will help ensure that your obligations are paid, which is essential to remaining in business. Some of these cash management principles are discussed below.

Getting Paid ASAP

Get paid as soon as you can without alienating customers. This is another one of those things that seems almost too obvious to mention, but experience tells me that it does indeed need mentioning. Too many small business people are just too patient or too laid back about collecting the money due them. The sooner you are paid, the sooner you have money to pay your own expenses *and* pay yourself. Further, the longer it takes to get paid, the more likely it is that you won't get paid at all. Statistically, an invoice that was issued only 20 days ago but not yet paid is considerably more likely to be paid at some point than one issued 90 days ago that hasn't yet been paid.

If you can be paid before you have to pay expenses connected with a particular sale, you then have the ability to earn money on the customer's money that you are temporarily holding. This practice, called *earning money on the float,* merely involves investing the cash you're paid in a secure interest-bearing investment, such as a money market account, until the time that you actually need it. Even though the earnings are generally small, they are easy earnings. In some cases, on the other hand, they can be substantial, even for very small companies such as those that deal with big-ticket items. For example, a contractor who manages construction of a house may be charging $150,000 to complete a job and may anticipate paying out $115,000 to carpenters, electricians, materials vendors, and the like. Ostensibly, his anticipated earnings are $35,000 for the completed project. However, if the entire project takes a year to complete, and the contractor is diligently billing his client to be $25,000 on average ahead in terms of collecting versus disbursing cash, he can earn an extra $1,250 on that cash over the year (assuming 5 percent interest).

Make It Easy for Customers to Pay You

Gone are the days when cash or checks were almost the only way for customers to pay the money they owed. Credit cards have now become popular, not only for retail and consumer transactions, but also for business-to-business transactions and, in fact, for just about any type of service. A few years ago, it would have been unheard of for a self-employed piano teacher or graphic designer to accept credit cards. Now, doing so is hardly a rarity and, I think, not doing so will soon be the exception. In order to accept credit cards, you have to set up a merchant account, which requires a certain expense and adherence to policies skewed to the advantage of credit card processors, but the advantage can be well worth it, as discussed in the following section.

Despite the convenience and immense popularity of credit cards and the venerability of cash and checks, still more options for payment exist today. Money can be wire transferred directly from one account to another through banks worldwide, a popular option for doing business internationally. Receiving wire transfers is as easy as supplying your account number, bank name, and bank routing number (which you can get from your bank) to the customers who want to pay this way. Payment is received into your account a few hours from the time it is sent, and once in your account you needn't worry about the payment bouncing or being stopped by the payer.

Payment systems based on the Internet are emerging such as Pay Pal, a system that conveniently combines credit card and wire transfer <www.paypal.com>. The more payment methods that you are set up to use, the better off you are. Offering an array of payment options will typically ensure you're paid earlier and will procure customers you may otherwise lose. The lesson here is simple: make it easy for your customers to pay you and you'll get payments more quickly.

Accepting Credit Cards

To be able to accept credit card payments, you must be set up with a credit card processing company or a bank that does its own processing. In general, only larger banks offer their own credit card processing services, but most commercial banks have referral arrangements with processors, so your bank would be a good first step for getting set up as a *merchant* that accepts cards. You can contact processing firms directly too. See your local Yellow Page directory under the heading "Credit Card and Other Plans Equipment, Supplies, and Services." Or a Web search using a term like "credit card processing services" will yield lots of possibilities.

All processors, whether bank owned or not, charge transaction fees for their service. You'll pay a percentage of each credit card sale (typically between 1 to 5 percent) as well as several other annoyance fees with euphemistic names like interchange fees, statement fees, and equipment fees. It would probably be more honest on the part of the banks and processors if they named these fees something like "charges we find we can get away with," but they won't. The percentage fees and annoyance fees do vary, so it wouldn't hurt to shop around. Unfortunately, though, most lifestyle businesses are not prize customers for processors, so they aren't in strong negotiating positions. Processors make their money primarily on the percentage charge for each sale, so large-volume customers are best from their perspective. Also, from a processor's perspective, larger average sales are better than smaller average sales because the effort involved in a transaction is much the same whether the transaction is $12 or $1,200.

You will be compelled to follow rules set forth by the credit card processors. For example, you will have to agree that you will charge no more for credit card sales than for sales by any other payment method. Also, your customers have the right to contest charges, and, based on certain policies, you'll have to accept the credit card processors' decrees about refunding to customers who demand refunds. In fact, your credit card processor will almost certainly have access to your business checking account and will deduct chargebacks as it deems appropriate. On most sales where you don't have a signature and a card swipe (virtually all phone, mail, and Web orders), you have almost no chance of winning a credit card dispute if the customer is persistent in challenging the charge.

What I'm telling you is that by accepting cards, you'll have to accept policies you may not like; you'll have to pay a percentage of each credit sale to a faceless company somewhere; you'll have to grant that faceless company access to your business checking account; and you'll have to pay fees that I derogatorily label as "annoyance fees." You also may well have to submit to filling out forms and other unplesantries to get set up in the first place. So why do it?

First is the previously discussed fact that it is to your advantage to offer customers a variety of choices for paying you. You'll be paid faster on the whole, and your rate of bad debt (not getting paid at all) will be lower.

Second, it becomes the bank's problem whether your customer (the bank's credit card holder) ever pays the charge. When and even whether the customer pays his credit card bill, you are paid through an automatic deposit to your account within a few days of the time the charge was made.

And third, it's a statistical fact that people are more likely to spend more if they can use a credit card. They are more likely to spring for the more expensive product or service, add the suggested accessories, and so on if they are using plastic.

So despite the fact that accepting cards is expensive, that you have to follow rules imposed by the processor and credit card company, and that you may lose an occasional payment that is legitimately due you, the benefits far outweigh the disadvantages for most businesses.

Paying Your Bills

My advice regarding paying your business bills (accounts payable) is pretty much the opposite of the advice I offered for getting paid. Whereas my advice on the latter was to get paid as soon as possible, my advice on the former is to pay on time but not before that. Just as you have use of your customer's money when you receive it, you have the use of your supplier's money until you pay.

Besides losing the use of that money when you pay early, you run the risk of getting your supplier accustomed to an early payment pattern, which can work to your disadvantage. Suppose, for example, you engage a Web developer to maintain your Web site.

Each month he sends you a bill with terms specified as "net 30 days," and you pay that bill 5 to 7 days after receiving it. Suppose that one month you are a bit strapped for cash so you don't pay in your usual prompt fashion but decide to wait a few weeks. Now had you always paid 25 to 30 days after the receipt of the bill, paying in 29 days would seem quite normal and expected. However, if all of a sudden your payment wasn't received in the usual 5 to 7 days, it could arouse suspicion, ill will, and even hesitance to do the work you need during your cash-strapped month(s). Don't allow your supplier to become accustomed to early payment.

Paying Bills with Credit Cards

Credit cards, long established as a convenient payment method for consumer purchases, are becoming increasingly popular for business-to-business purchases as well, as noted above.

The advantages of accepting credit payments were also covered above, and there are good reasons to pay your business expenses by credit as well. For one thing, you are given payment credit by your vendor when you make the transaction, but you have anywhere from a few days to a month or more (depending on where in your billing cycle the transaction is made) before you actually have to pay the charge with *real* dollars. You can take better advantage of the grace period by making the transaction soon after your statement's closing date. For example, suppose your Visa statement's closing date is the 6th of the month, and you charge something on April 8th. You won't be billed until your May statement, and depending on the grace period policies of the bank issuing your card, you won't be required to pay for up to several weeks after receipt of the May statement. So you may get nearly two months of interest-free money based on the grace period. Be very careful playing this game though. If you wait too long to pay, you'll be hit with high interest charges and probably with late fees as well, wiping out the advantage of the grace period and then some.

Now you can, of course, use your credit card to get a quick and convenient loan by making less than the full payment. As convenient as this form of business borrowing is, it is also very expensive—credit card interest rates are quite high. With appropriate caution, this is a reasonable method of obtaining emergency and occasional small loans. Using credit cards for business loans is covered in more detail in Chapter 6.

Ideally, you should have a separate credit card for business use and should avoid the same card for business and personal use. This doesn't mean one card has to be in the name of your business but only that it should be limited to business purchases, which makes for cleaner recordkeeping. Also, the IRS doesn't require a separate business credit card, but it will make your life easier to have one in case you face an audit. Otherwise, you may have to do a lot more untangling of business and personal expenses and proving the accuracy of your untangling.

The Fixed-Overhead Trap

Overhead expenses are fixed expenses that must be paid periodically (typically monthly) regardless of how many sales you're making or how much money you're taking in. Your monthly phone bill, rent, and perhaps Internet service provider fees are examples of overhead expenses.

Variable costs, on the other hand, are directly related to sales and are such expenses as the actual inventory you're reselling, sales commissions, delivery expenses, and other expenses that vary with the amount of goods or services that are being sold. Variable costs, if you are purchasing wisely and keeping good controls, are an acceptable and necessary element of business. They are driven by sales, so when variable costs increase, it is because sales too are increasing. If your sales go down, variable costs also drop proportionally.

Overhead costs, even though necessary to a degree, can be dangerous if not closely monitored and controlled. A company with a high overhead can get into trouble easily if it has a few lean months, because those overhead expenses must be paid regardless of monthly sales levels.

Traditional advice for entrepreneurs holds that a business should grow and growth requires overhead. At the same time, keeping up with new overhead requires that growth continue. A bigger factory needs more orders to support its overhead, and a service company that hires more employees needs paying work to keep those employees busy enough to earn their keep. Traditional advice continues that even though management should only take on overhead that is necessary and affordable, overcautiousness limits growth, and growth is a prime element of successful business. So long as the business can support the overhead, there won't be a financial problem.

The lifestyle business, however, may have a problem that goes beyond the financial. Even though you may be able to support a larger overhead and an expanded company, doing so may be incongruent with your lifestyle aspirations. Suppose, for example, two companies are in the business of making children's clothing. One is a traditional company whose owner's aspiration is to expand and eventually become a multi-million-dollar manufacturer. The other is a lifestyle entrepreneur who wants to work only during school hours so she can earn an income but still be available to her kids after school.

To the first business owner, buying new equipment, hiring employees, or moving to a larger facility would be feasible and logical as soon as it was financially practical. To the second, though, taking on this kind of overhead, even if financially viable, might jeopardize the whole reason the business was launched in the first place.

Well-Considered Growth

Few businesses should or could eliminate overhead completely. However, it is important to keep your fixed recurring costs in alignment not only with your finances but with your reasons for having a business. In Chapter 2, I suggested that you consider the ways in which your proposed business would enable rather than impede your lifestyle goals.

Successful businesses are usually faced with seductive growth opportunities that involve adding to overhead by either buying more equipment, hiring more personnel, or otherwise adding to their infrastructure. What is an opportunity for most businesses can be a trap to the lifestyle entrepreneur; the opportunity to expand on one's creation is truly seductive, for not only can it validate its creator's concept but it can add to its creator's status and wealth. It can be so seductive that it can blind lifestyle entrepreneurs to the fact that their lifestyle goal was to take long trips or practice their profession in a unique and personal way.

I'm not saying growth is bad, because business growth is usually good. What is not so good is growth that is inconsistent with the objectives of the business and its owner. In my role as a business broker, I always ask prospective sellers why they want to sell their company. About 10 percent of the time, the answer is like this: "The business just got away from me. I started it because I wanted to (run a gallery, work one-on-one with clients, design Web sites, etc.), and now I'm spending 14 hours a day managing a business and not enjoying it."

I am currently working on the sale of a company owned by a software engineer who started a very successful company that sells software products of his design. Why does he want to sell? He started the business because he wanted to spend his time creating software, but he now spends 85 percent of his time on sales, management, and finance. Now he wants to sell to someone who will take responsibility for running the company and hire him to write software full-time.

If taking on new overhead will enhance your business *and* is consistent with your lifestyle goals, by all means do it. But don't take on overhead you can't afford or overhead you can afford but would threaten the lifestyle that your business is designed to enable.

Dealing with Taxes

Hundreds of books are written about strategies for minimizing taxes, and many professionals devote their entire careers to assisting business owners in tax planning. Obviously, the entire field can't be covered in this book, but lifestyle entrepreneurs and other self-employed persons should give some thought to planning for (read minimizing) taxes.

Many lifestyle business owners more or less ignore the issue of taxation, reasoning that tax strategies are for bigger business where thousands or millions of dollars are at stake. I argue the reverse. Large public companies work with what is called *OPM*—other people's money. If such a company pays the government a few thousand dollars more than it could have had its tax planning been more advantageous, the damage is minor for the company's owners (its shareholders). On the other hand, self-employed people and small business owners have to wring the maximum out of each dollar. The self-employed who pay a few hundred dollars more than necessary in taxes see their own income decrease by that same amount. To a very small business, a few tax mistakes can jeopardize the entire business.

One way lifestyle entrepreneurs unnecessarily lose a lot of money that could go into their pockets is through carelessness that results in tax penalties and interest. The IRS and virtually every other taxing authority set and clearly state due dates for the various taxes they collect. If those dates are missed by as little as a day, the taxing authority can and will hit you with a stiff penalty of 5 percent or more; a few days late can mean a 10 percent penalty. On top of the penalty, you'll be assessed an interest charge for late payments. The antidote to late-payment penalties and interest charges is another one of those things that seems too obvious to mention, but experience has taught me that it does need pointing out: *pay your taxes on time!*

Too many entrepreneurs just don't want to deal with taxes. Letters from taxing authorities containing notices of taxes due and intimidating-looking forms are put aside and even left unopened until it's too late to respond without accruing a penalty.

Many entrepreneurs fall into this tax trap: They miss a payment date and hear nothing from the taxing authority. Then they miss another and still nothing. They naively convince themselves that maybe the tax isn't really due or at least the taxing authority is being kind and letting them put it off until they are in better shape financially. Then all of a sudden they're called or visited by an IRS officer demanding payment, including penalties and interest, within ten days and outlining the rights of the IRS to compel payment, including attaching bank accounts, seizing property, and related unpleasantries provided by law. This is a particularly likely scenario in the case of a failure to pay taxes due that were withheld (or should have been withheld) from employee payrolls, but the scenario is not limited to withholding taxes.

Complying with Tax Regulations

Most working Americans work for an employer. And that employer is responsible for withholding a prescribed amount of money from each employee each time a paycheck is written and then turning over that money (and more) to the government.

Self-employed people and other business owners, though, are responsible for periodically paying the government directly for the taxes they owe. In fact, small business owners with employees must take responsibility for withholding money from employees and paying it to the government.

As with taxes in general, the best recommendations I can offer is to consult an accountant regarding the taxes you'll owe and when you'll need to pay them. Having said that, following are some of the taxes you'll be responsible for and the requisite reporting and payment requirements.

Income Taxes

If you're employed, whether self-employed, employed by a large organization, or employed by a business you own, you will most likely owe income taxes on your earnings to the U.S. government. In many states, you'll owe state income taxes as well.

If you're employed by an organization, that organization is responsible for withholding money from your wages and periodically paying into the government on your behalf. If you are an employer, you are responsible for withholding money from employees' wages, even if you are the sole employee of your company. The self-employed, too, are responsible for making periodic payments of income taxes due the government.

Social Security and Medicare Taxes

Earnings from salary, wages, and tips (not profits or dividends) are subject to Social Security taxes and Medicare taxes. As of this writing (late 2002), employees must pay 6.2 percent of their earnings for Social Security taxes (for the first $84,900 of income each year) and 1.45 percent of earnings for Medicare taxes (for their entire income each year). Many employees don't understand that their employers are required to match their payments dollar for dollar, such that the government gets twice as much as each employee pays in.

In the case of the self-employed, there is no employer to pay the other half, so self-employed people are responsible for paying a *self-employment tax* as their contribution to Social Security and Medicare. The amount due for each self-employed person is almost the same as the total due for an employee's earnings (employer and employee contribution combined).

Unemployment Taxes

Employers (even those who employ only themselves through a corporate entity) generally must pay into their state's unemployment insurance fund. Rates vary depending on the state, industry, previous claim record, and more. Sole proprietors must pay unemployment taxes for their employees but not for themselves.

Sales Tax

In many states, businesses that sell tangible goods must charge a sales tax on those goods and pay that tax to the state government. In general, services are not taxable for sales tax purposes, but check with your accountant to be sure. In some cases where you're providing a service that includes a product, the whole fee is taxable. For example, suppose you are a filmmaker who just produced a film for a client and billed that client $6,000 for the finished film. Even though the raw film you used and delivered to the client was only worth, say, $40, your entire bill may be subject to sales tax in some states because it is a tangible product.

Property Taxes

In some states and cites, anything owned by a business, including equipment and inventory, is taxable property for which the business is liable. Of course, automobile and real estate owners are liable for property tax just about everywhere.

Periodic Payments

People who are self-employed (virtually anyone who is personally receiving payment without taxes withheld) must generally pay estimated taxes to the IRS on a quarterly basis. Mathematicians might challenge the term *quarterly,* because for some inexplicable reason these taxes are not due at equal three-month intervals throughout the year. They are due on April 15 for the first calendar quarter, June 15 for the second calendar quarter, September 15 for the third calendar quarter, and January 15 for the fourth calendar quarter (of the preceding year).

The idea is to pay along the way so that you'll owe a small balance or be owed a small refund by the IRS for the year. In most cases, penalties are assessed for significant underpayment (though no rewards for overpayment).

Most states that have an income tax require quarterly estimated payments as well, usually on the same schedule as the IRS.

Employee taxes and incorporated businesses. If you are being paid by a corporation, even if you are its sole owner and sole employee, you must withhold taxes and pay them to the government on a different schedule. Depending on the total dollar amount withheld from employees, payments may be due quarterly, monthly, or more frequently.

Tax forms. Almost all taxes due must be paid with an accompanying form detailing how the amount was computed, what it is for, and so on. In several instances, the form is due on a regular basis even if no taxes are due.

If you register as a business entity, such as a corporation or an LLC, both the state taxing authorities where you register and the IRS will learn of your existence and send you the appropriate forms. You can also download the federal (IRS) forms from the IRS Web site at <www.irs.gov>. Tax forms for most states are available at each state's Web site. All 50 states' Web sites can be accessed on the Web using this format: <www.state.(state's 2-digit postal code).us>. For example, for New York go to <www.state.ny.us>, for Texas <www.state.tx.us>, and so on.

If you are operating as a sole proprietorship (or otherwise not forming an entity that is registered with a state), you must obtain at least the appropriate forms for paying periodic self-employment taxes and estimated withholding taxes. The forms can be obtained from the Web (see above), but it is best to check with your accountant who will be familiar with your overall tax situation.

Consulting an accountant. Unless you're familiar with the various federal, local, and state tax regulations as they apply to business (and if you are, chances are you're not reading this section), it is important to consult an accountant regarding the taxes for which you'll be responsible and their due dates. An accountant can also show you how to fill out the forms and remain in compliance with the various taxing authorities. A good accountant can help you minimize taxes due by making suggestions about the financial aspects of your business.

Deductible Expenses and Capital Expenditures

A key tenet of business taxation is that business expenses are deductible—that is, business expenses can be deducted from business income before computing the taxable amount of income. If you took in $50,000 last year and had business expenses such as advertising, telephone, office supplies, business travel, and so on of $30,000, you earned $20,000 ($50,000–$30,000).

The IRS and other taxing authorities give business owners a good deal of latitude in determining what kind of business expenses are reasonable. In general, if you have a good reason for spending money for business purposes, seldom will the IRS challenge that expense. You won't hear an IRS agent asking if you could have saved money on airfare by staying over a Saturday night or if you could have shopped around for a cheaper long-distance service. Within reason, you can decide how best to spend money for business purposes without worrying that the IRS will question your judgment.

The IRS and other taxing authorities do require proof, however, that you actually did spend the money you said you spent for business purposes. It is therefore essential that you keep records of all your business expenses and retain receipts and invoices for those expenses. You probably don't need a complex system to manage these receipts and invoices. All that is required is a system whereby you can retrieve those little pieces of paper if you're called on to do so, as you might be in a tax audit. For example, a simple accordion folder with separated sections for each month's invoices and receipts should suffice for smaller businesses. Though such a system is simple, if you need to find a certain invoice, it is a merely a matter of going to the appropriate month's section of the folder and searching through that section Yes, you may be putting these little pieces of paper in the accordion folder and never look at them again, but if you're ever called to document your expenses (audited), your proof will be findable, and you'll save a lot of time, money, and aggravation.

U.S. tax laws differentiate between expenses for things that are used by a business over a relatively short period of time, things bought and resold (inventory), and things bought by the business and expected to last for more than a year. Things used for a short period of time are categorized as business expenses and can generally be deducted from income in the year they are purchased.

Items that have a longer useful life and therefore retain part of their value, such as computers, automobiles, and other business equipment, can not be *expensed* in the year they are purchased (with an important exception explained below). The rules are arcane and the result of political compromises. Basically, such goods must be expensed or *written off* over a few years, though typically over fewer years than the items actually last. The concept is called *accelerated depreciation,* meaning that even though you can't deduct them in a single year, you can deduct them over fewer years than their actual life. A car may last five to ten years, but according to IRS rules it generally can be fully deducted over a much shorter period of time. To make it even more complicated, such items are not depreciated equally over the number of years allowed, but the depreciation is front-loaded instead, which allows you to take more of a depreciation (more business expense) in the early years of that item's useful life.

The government offers a little gift to small business when it comes to capital expenditures. The first $25,000 (as of 2003) of capital expenditure can be expensed in the year of purchase. So if you buy computer equipment, furniture, and/or any other business equipment (as usual, with some exceptions), you can treat the purchase as a business expense and take the full deduction in the year of purchase up to $25,000. The government is in essence chipping in with you toward the purchase of equipment by giving you a benefit at tax time. The government does draw a line however. You can only use this Section 179 deduction against profits; you can't use it to generate a loss (though the unused portion can be carried forward to the next tax year). Check with your accountant when making a major purchase.

Timing of Business Purchases

The timing of purchases can make a real difference in the amount of taxes you'll pay and the dates when tax payments are due. Assuming your business uses *cash basis accounting*, which almost all self-employed people and lifestyle entrepreneurs do, the clock is set back to zero and restarted at the beginning of each year. Thus, if you pay a bill on December 31 (assuming your business is run on a calendar year) even though whatever you bought will be used entirely in the following year, it is a business expense in the year it was purchased and a tax deduction in that year. On the other hand, if you get a big check from a client in December for work to be done in January and February, it is income in the earlier year even though you'll face expenses associated with that income in the next year.

To some degree you can take advantage of a new year's restarting of the tax clock. For example, many small businesses stock up and pay for supplies in December and even pay some bills in advance. That way, they can take the tax deduction in the year the purchases were made and thereby lowering taxes due for that year. One qualifier: You can't prepay expenses for which you haven't yet been billed, though it is okay to ask a vendor to send a bill a bit early.

Also, if you decide in December that you need two items, each costing $20,000, and assuming you haven't bought any other capital equipment that year, you can save a lot of money by buying one item in December and the other in January of the next year. That way you can deduct the full expenditure as an expense (half in each year, assuming no other capital purchases in either year).

Confused? If you're new to accounting and tax law, I'm sure this sounds a bit surreal—and, believe me, I've just scratched the surface. Nevertheless, it is the way the tax code works and is probably the way it will work for the foreseeable future. Silly as the laws may seem, using them effectively can be one of those survival skills that helps a small business succeed.

Rather than learning the arcane tax code, consult an accountant to find the most appropriate tax strategy in your particular situation, and consult that accountant every time you plan to make a major purchase—he or she may have a suggestion that can save you hundreds of dollars in taxes. With the guidance of a good accountant, you can learn to use the tax laws to your own financial advantage—and do it legally.

A recommended book on taxes for small business is *Tax Savvy for Small Business: Year-Round Tax Strategies to Save You Money,* by Frederick W. Daily (Nolo, 2002).

Summary

It's fair to say that most lifestyle entrepreneurs find little thrill in financial management or tax planning. This book is addressed to people looking to small business as an enabling vehicle for pursuing interests other than business itself and certainly other than those mundane aspects of business management. In fact, I fear that many of my readers' eyes have glazed over well before now in this chapter.

Financial and tax management need not be central to your life nor even to your business. Nevertheless, you do have to pay attention to these aspects of your business. Not doing so will at best lower your income and at worst jeopardize your business and your overall financial well-being.

The advice of an accountant is crucial in determining which taxes you are responsible for and when they are due. Accountants can also advise on tax planning and financial management strategies, but the day-to-day financial management responsibilities fall to you as the business owner. Educating yourself in the principles of managing your money and mastering tax issues that directly affect you will undoubtedly pay dividends.

CHAPTER

10

Setting Priorities and Managing Time

Managing Time

Time is your most important asset. We hear statements like this so often that they've become clichés. Nevertheless, in the case of running your own business, the cliché is also the reality.

Lots of big companies sponsor internal and external public relations campaigns touting such slogans as "Our people are our most important asset" or "Our people make our company great." In reality, though, it would be a rare electric utility that values employees more than it values a generating plant and a rare manufacturing company that considers its employees more valuable than a factory. Despite the PR, most employees are seen as replaceable commodities. People come first only to the extent that the company finds their labor and services cost efficient.

It's not that corporate managers are mean-spirited. The stated purpose of large companies is to increase the value of stocks for shareholders, not to provide fulfilling jobs for their employees. A CEO can't expect kudos at the annual meeting by explaining: "Even though your stock is worth half what you paid for it, we're successful because we kept all our employees employed and happy despite the loss of your money."

It's different for small private companies that don't have to worry about pleasing shareholders, at least not shareholders who aren't intimately involved with the business.

For a self-employed person and most owners of lifestyle companies, people really are the most important asset. This is not to imply that entrepreneurs are morally superior. Rather, people are essential to these businesses on two levels. First, the business exists for the lifestyle benefit of its owner (who may be the only employee or one of a very few). Second, the service being offered is based largely, if not entirely, on the skills and talents of the person or persons behind the company. In the case of the electric utility, for example, the service being sold is more the result of a large asset the company owns (electric-generating facilities) than of the people it employs.

If several longtime electric company employees left their job, the company would still produce its service in the same way; the same is true for a large manufacturing company. If a lifestyle business that offers piano lessons, Web design services, or consulting, on the other hand, lost its employee(s), the business would continue in a very different fashion if it were to continue at all. The business itself is truly a manifestation of the person or persons behind it.

Larger companies, especially public companies, strive to break away from the idea that the business is a reflection of its people. The best scenario for most larger companies is one in which the company is successfully able to operate regardless of the specific personalities involved. Ideally, in large company logic, personnel will come and go to fill the needed slots, but the company will transcend the people filling the slots. Changes in top management undoubtedly affect the company, but even top managers are seen as stewards of the organization, which is a greater whole than the current people running it.

Prioritizing Your Time

One of the hardest things to get used to for new graduates of large organizations moving to entrepreneurship is their now having to make all the decisions about their own time allocation. No authority is assigning projects or doing anything else to budget their time for them. It is incredibly easy to abdicate your time management responsibility by letting the most immediate demand take priority over endeavors that might be more important.

To say you're in charge of your time now sounds like another empty cliché, but it isn't. How you manage this limited and most important asset of your business will have a major impact on its success. You must determine overall priorities and structure your time to effectively deal with those priorities. For example, suppose you are a Web designer specializing in Web sites for health-related companies. You're working on two proposals for prospective clients, either one of which could not only keep you busy for six months but also set the stage for a good deal of future work and set your company on the path you envision for it. Suppose further that you're strapped for cash. Now suppose while you're working on these two proposals, your former employer calls to ask you to develop a Web site right away—he needs it within three weeks—and promises to pay your rate (at the high end). Doing this job will bring in needed cash, but it won't help you toward your long-term goals in the health care marketplace and in fact might jeopardize your chances of getting the important proposals submitted on time.

Do you put aside the proposal and create the Web site for your former employer? After all, it's a definite job and quick cash. Or do you say no thanks and stay on course with your proposals? No easy answer. The best is that you have to make a decision in line with your own priorities as you've determined them, which often means balancing short-term needs against long-term goals.

Reasonable people could argue for either option in this example, but I've seen many entrepreneurs lose sight of priorities in far less doubtful situations. Too often, people feel they must respond to the most salient issue, the one right in front of them, and not the most important one. I've seen people put aside essential projects to deal with issues of decidedly less importance. In an extreme example, I once learned a client of mine missed an important client meeting because he just had to make sure the new video card he installed on his computer was working properly (he saw the card was working but lost his client). I've seen business owners get so upset about not being paid that they've spent hours working on collecting small amounts of money when their time is desperately needed in areas of far more importance than a few dollars.

You must prioritize your goals and translate those goals into steps that need doing. Decide what steps are of primary and secondary importance followed by those of lesser importance. I like to use an *ABC List, A* being essential things to do, *B* important but less than essential, and *C* things worth doing if there's time. Once priorities are in order, they can be used to evaluate the inevitable crises and situations that come up, and you can decide whether they really do merit your attention and time or whether they are mere distractions vis-à-vis in terms of your goals and priorities.

Organizational Geniuses

While working with some very successful entrepreneurs of the traditional school, I've asked a number of them to what they attribute their entrepreneurial success. Several answered that they are unusually smart marketers, and others credit their good ideas or their superior creative abilities for their success. Still others talk about their mastery of finance and deal making.

Frankly, not all of them are as superior as they think they are in marketing, creativity, or finance. I have, however, noticed one overall characteristic that most of these successful entrepreneurs do possess, even though few of them recognize it. They are very good at prioritizing and organizing; their desks and offices may be messy and appear disorganized, but their minds are not. They think in terms of priorities and goals, dividing those goals into short-term, medium-term, and long-term goals, and they're not easily distracted from those priorities and goals despite day-to-day crises, brush fires, and opportunities.

These entrepreneurs fully believe that their time is the most important asset of their business, and they prioritize and utilize their time judiciously. I once had a client who fit the successful entrepreneur profile to a tee; he kept a detailed schedule book three years in advance with the third year partially filled with specific projects, tasks, and appointments!

Psychologists might have a less-than-complimentary term for a person who plans his life with such precision so far in advance. I'm not suggesting that lifestyle entrepreneurs must be as obsessed with time management as this client of mine. I am suggesting, though, that you do have to structure and allocate your time with care. There is an undeniable correlation between time management and business success.

To some people, managing time in view of set goals comes quite naturally. If you're one of these people, you probably don't need my advice in this area. To many others though, time management requires a new framework and a degree of discipline. If you're of the latter school, it is worth training yourself to think in terms of priorities and specific goals and developing the mind-set to plan your time to meet those priorities and goals.

An excellent book on the subject of time management is *The Personal Efficiency Program: How to Get Organized to Do More Work in Less Time* (*2d Edition*), by Kerry Gleeson (John Wiley, 2000).

Real Work

A former client of mine, an engineer, started a business to design and build specialized industrial machinery. He once commented to me: "With managing finances, customer meetings, putting together promotional materials, and all that, I hardly have time to do the real work." As far as he was concerned the only "real work" was designing and building machines. Marketing and business management to him were annoyances at best or necessary evils at worst.

Many highly skilled professionals share this attitude. After all, if you went to school for years to learn a profession, it may seem somehow undesirable, perhaps even demeaning, to spend work time on matters of running a small business. However, to run a business, no matter how small, you need to do just that—run the business. If allocating time to business management is too distasteful, you probably shouldn't be in business for yourself. In spite of several advantages of being on your own, one of the disadvantages (at least as some people see it) is that you need to spend some of your time managing and planning that business, even if it means taking time away from practicing the profession for which you were trained.

A business needs overall direction and goals along the way. In a small business, owners who are setting the direction are also implementing the plan to get there by meeting the goals they set. Although it may seem a contradiction, the day-to-day work of the business can too easily obstruct the goals and jeopardize the overall direction owners seek. You need to balance doing the work for which your business exists with maintaining your overall plan.

Flexibility in Time Management

Now for the disclaimer: Every entrepreneur seems to understand well the saying that "when you're up to your ass in alligators, it's hard to remember that your goal was to drain the swamp."

Entrepreneurship involves entering uncharted territory. Doing so means that by its very nature, unexpected things will happen. You can't possibly plan your time with complete precision when you don't know the exact direction a business will take or what demands on your time will be made and what brush fires will break out. You do know, however, that brush fires will break out, and at least a few unexpected things will happen.

Though underplanning is more of an issue with lifestyle entrepreneurs than is overplanning, the latter is still a danger. Actually, the problem isn't so much overplanning as overadherence to a plan when it becomes out of sync with reality. Though I insist planning is important, I also admit that I've never seen a business that was able to stay with its initial plan without significant modifications along the way. Planning is an essential part of starting a business, but so is the flexibility to vary from the plan in the face of dynamic situational realities.

So make your plans, set your goals, and prioritize your time. But don't become a slave to your plans and goals. Maintain enough flexibility to vary the plan and modify it in the face of day-to-day business realities.

CHAPTER

11

The New Enablers of Lifestyle Business

Some of the changes we've seen over the past several years have made it easier to choose lifestyle entrepreneurship. Many of the major and most obvious changes have been in the realm of technology, particularly in personal technology. Less glitzy enablers of lifestyle entrepreneurship are such commonplace modern services as overnight package delivery and office superstores.

This chapter outlines these modern small business enablers and explains how you can use them to your advantage.

Technology

Businesses of all sizes are budgeting and spending lots of money on technology accompanied by the emergence of new and well-used phrases such as *technology infrastructure* and *systems integration.* Although some of the spending is for current needs, much of it is also viewed as an investment in a future that will be more and more technology based. Companies that are not at the cutting edge of technology, the reasoning goes, will be in a progressively weaker position relative to their more technologically competent competitors. To a large degree this is true; businesses that don't integrate technology may well have difficulty surviving a few years down the line.

To the lifestyle business, technology is even more important than it is to other businesses. If I claim the very long-term survival of many businesses depends on integrating technology, how can I also claim technology is more important to the lifestyle entrepreneur? How can technology be more important to a self-employed piano teacher and an architectural consultant whose professions were practiced well before anyone heard of a computer? Well, technology is the very enabler of many lifestyle businesses. Much of this technology makes it feasible to work at one's chosen hours, at home, or even at no fixed location. Many thriving lifestyle companies today could not have existed before voice mail, computers, and other technology became readily available.

There was a time (that yours truly remembers) when a phone would just keep right on ringing if no one was there to pick it up. Now, answering machines and their modern cousin, voice mail, may not seem like high-tech wonders. But until they were available, there wasn't an easy and reliable way to leave a message for someone short of leaving that message with another human being. A self-employed person unavailable to answer the phone during business hours was at a major disadvantage. Now that answering devices are ubiquitous (despite the fact that people love to say they hate them, they accept them), they help to make lifestyle entrepreneurship possible.

Answering devices are just the beginning. Fax machines are an amazing convenience for any business and a godsend for self-employed people who may not have assistants or time to run a document to a client across town.

Computers, of course, make it possible to keep records and prepare professional-looking documents without bookkeepers or secretaries. They also allow efficient and cheap communication via e-mail as well as easy research and the purchase of supplies and services right from your desktop via the Web.

Even personal photocopiers, which weren't readily available until the mid-1980s, do their part to enable any room in the house to become a relatively modern office. Years ago, one needed a real office in an office building to efficiently conduct business, at least in most fields. The cost of needed equipment like copiers could not be justified unless it was shared by several users. Not so anymore.

Clearly, answering machines, photocopiers, and computers have made many more areas (like spare bedrooms and finished basements) suitable small business offices. Now, other devices such as cellular phones, laptop computers, and personal digital assistants (PDAs) are in some cases making offices unnecessary at all. At the least, the reach of the office has been extended so that one can do work on a laptop from anywhere, communicate by phone from anywhere, and even retrieve voice mail or answering machine messages from anywhere.

What's more, most of this enabling technology is relatively cheap. At this writing, a personal computer with modem and printer can be had for about $1,000. For just a few hundred dollars more, add a basic fax machine, a personal photocopier, and an answering machine (or skip the answering machine and get voice mail instead for a few dollars per month). In fact, you can even save a few dollars by buying an all-in-one scanner, photocopier, and fax machine.

Client Expectations

Perhaps you're convinced that you can get by just fine without any of this office technology. Perhaps you never send faxes and never have to write so much as a business letter or an e-mail. Maybe you are always around or you have others answer your phone if you're not.

In the unlikely event that this is the case, I'll still argue that you need a few basic tech items. In this 21st century, it is pretty much assumed that telephones, fax machines, and computers are part of any business, no matter how small. Every prospective client is sizing you up when making an inquiry. If that prospect asks for an e-mail address and you have to admit you don't use e-mail, you have just lost points in that prospect's mind. Not only does it make the prospect question the reason why you don't use this most basic service, it also denies her a favored way to communicate with you (we know she favors it because otherwise she wouldn't have asked for your e-mail address in the first place). Likewise, when a prospective client requests you fax a proposal or informs you he'll fax you information, he doesn't want to hear you don't have a fax machine, regardless of the reason. Fax machines, too, are so integrated into modern business that not having one puts you at a disadvantage.

What Do You Need?

Tech needs, of course, differ from business to business. If you're a Web developer, a freelance software developer, or a network engineer, by all means skip right over this section because it doesn't apply to you. You need more technology, and you know what you need. The rudimentary technology list that I outline here is for businesses that aren't selling technology-oriented services.

Essentials

These are the most basic technology equipment and services that most any business needs.

Computer and peripherals. A desktop computer is almost essential for everything from composing and printing a business letter to sending a bill and using e-mail and the Web. Although there is virtually no difference between a computer called a small business computer and one called a home computer, there is a difference in the software bundled with each. Home computers come with preinstalled games and other family-oriented software. Business computers come with basic business software, which is what you need.

The current standard in business software is Microsoft Office, so if you're buying a new machine, try to get one bundled with this software. Cheaper models often come with Microsoft Works, which is okay but not as good as Office. If you buy a computer without Office installed, or if you're using a home computer that doesn't have Office software installed, my advice is to invest in the Office package. Not only does it do the jobs it's intended to do very well, but it is the business standard, meaning that you'll be able to share files with other businesses—that is, you'll be able to send and receive documents by e-mail and so on. Different versions of Office vary as to what is included, but all current versions include word processing software (Word), spreadsheet software (Excel), and e-mail and information management software (Outlook). The more expensive versions (Microsoft Professional) also include database management software (Access), presentation software (Powerpoint), and even desktop publishing software (Publisher).

You don't need a top-of-the-line computer for basic business applications. Virtually any modern computer will do for lifestyle businesses and most very small companies. The exceptions would be companies involved in processing intensive endeavors, such as video editing or graphics, on a regular basis

Modem. A modem is a device that lets you communicate over phone lines. It is the most basic (and slowest method) for accessing the Internet. If you are doing a considerable amount of e-mailing or Web browsing, a *broadband* modem, either DSL or cable, is a must. Arguments are made pro and con for DSL versus cable, but both offer vastly superior Internet access than do telephone *dial-up modems;* most computers now come with a built-in dial-up modem. If you want high-speed access, you'll need a networking card too, which can be included with a new computer or added if your computer doesn't have one built in.

Printer. If you ever intend to print anything, you will of course need a printer. If you're printing a lot, say more than 15 or 20 pages a day on average, a laser printer is probably your best bet. Laser printers cost more, but they are much faster than other types of printers. Your other alternative is an inkjet printer. Inkjets are cheaper to buy but more expensive to operate because they use expensive inkjet cartridges. Although they're cheap and slow, the print quality is quite good. Unlike lower-priced laser printers, inkjet printers are capable of printing in color and most of them do quite a good job with color (though color printing is very slow).

You can buy a computer with Microsoft Office software, a modem, an inkjet printer, and more for about $1,000.

Internet service provider. Just as you need a phone company to use your telephone, you need an Internet service provider (ISP) to gain access to the Internet. Several hundred ISPs in this country offer dial-up access, some regional and others national. If you travel, a large national service (AOL, Earthlink, MSN) may be best because these national services have local access numbers from most cities. For broadband access, your provider choices are far fewer; you are generally limited to cable companies, phone companies, and a few of the larger ISPs, though options are increasing.

Fax machine. It's hard to do business without a fax machine. There are plain-paper models that cost a bit more than the special-paper models but are preferred because they offer more flexibility and better print quality. Fax machines can double as basic copy machines; if you need copies only on an occasional basis, a plain-paper fax machine may be good enough for your needs. But if you need more than two or three copies a day, I recommend a freestanding copier. Although plain-paper fax machines cost a bit more than the machines that use special paper, that special paper is fairly expensive. If you expect to receive more than three or four faxed pages a week, a plain-paper model will be cheaper in the long run.

You can use your computer as a fax machine, but I don't recommend it. Unless you have a scanner, you can send only documents by fax that you produced from your computer or received from another computer by disk, e-mail, download, and so on. With a scanner, you can scan non-computer-generated documents, but the scanning process is more time consuming than faxing from a dedicated fax machine. Finally, I've found fax software to be quirky and unreliable.

You can get a separate phone line for the fax. Many small businesses, in fact, get a single additional phone line that is shared by the fax and the modem, which means, of course, that you can't send or receive a fax while online. Some fax machines can distinguish between a phone call and a fax call and will switch automatically, making a shared voice and fax line practical for light use.

Answering machine/voice mail. Unless someone is available to answer the phone during normal business hours (at least), you need an inexpensive automatic answering device.

Alternatively, in most parts of the country now, you can obtain voice mail from your phone company. Voice mail is like an answering machine without the machine; a centralized computer somewhere other than at your office takes messages and allows you to retrieve them from any telephone at any time. The primary advantage of voice mail in comparison with answering machines is that voice mail will take a message even if you're on the phone on that line. With voice mail on a phone line, that line will never have busy signals. Phone companies tout voice mail—which adds a few dollars a month to your phone bill—by claiming it's more reliable than answering machines, though the reliability advantage is small in my experience. Both have occasional technical problems, although voice mail problems are fixed quickly and by someone else.

Other Telephone Features and Tricks

All the new "tricks" that telephones perform today add a few dollars to your monthly bill. Of three recent features, I like two for lifestyle businesses but one I very much recommend against.

Call forwarding. This feature lets you have calls to a particular phone line automatically forwarded to any other line. The caller doesn't know that the call to you in Chicago is being answered by you in your car, in your hotel room in New York, or at your cabin in the country. If you spend a lot of time away from the office, this is a nice feature.

Conference calling (3-way calling). This feature lets you have conference calls among several people at the same time. I use it a lot in my business-brokering activities to have buyer, seller, and myself meet via phone. If you foresee a use for conference calls, this is a good feature to have.

Call waiting. This is one of the worst telephone tricks ever invented. It's bad enough for household use but for business it's worse. First, it interrupts calls in progress. Even worse, if you respond to the interrupter, you're giving the message that there is someone more important on the other line. I advise passing on this feature.

Other Technology That Might Be Helpful

For most lifestyle businesses, the essential technology aids are detailed above. Additional equipment that could be helpful (essential in some situations) is explained below.

Cellular phones. Cell phones hardly need explanation. If you are away from your main phone a lot, a cell phone is essential. You can remain in contact with virtually anyone from virtually anywhere. You can even have calls forwarded from your main phone number to your cell phone if your phone company offers the call forwarding feature. The caller won't know whether you are in your office or 2,000 miles away because the forwarding of a call from your regular number is invisible. Some owners of part-time businesses rely on their cell phones while at their day jobs to avoid violating personal use of company phone policies at work.

Scanners. Scanners allow you to copy virtually any document into your computer and are very useful for adding pictures to documents. Software can recognize actual characters and translate the scanned document into computer-readable text. This kind of software has come a long way but is still less than perfect.

Photocopiers. The only reason that I didn't put this device in the essential group is that fax machines can double as simple copying machines. However, a freestanding copier is easier and faster to use and provides better copies.

PDAs (Palm Pilots, et al.). Personal digital assistants, or PDAs, do many things and will undoubtedly do more in the future. They are excellent for keeping addresses and phone numbers and as electronic appointment books. It's easier to carry around a three-by-five-inch PDA than an appointment book, address book, and several scraps of paper. PDAs do a lot of other things, too, ranging from playing games to keeping databases, expense records, and more. Higher-end models can even access the Internet (for which a monthly fee is charged). As this book goes to press, all-in-one combination units that include a PDA, Internet access, and cellular telephone capabilities are becoming popular. If you travel a lot and need many different kinds of information at your fingertips, a PDA might be very convenient, if not indispensable.

Technology Doesn't Make a Business

I've sung the praise of technology in this chapter, pointing out the conveniences and efficiencies it offers, marveled at how cheap it has become, and even called it an enabler of many types of lifestyle businesses. Yet I need to point out that technology in and of itself does not a business make. Some think of technology as an end in itself, which it may be in some situations, but business is not one of those situations. Don't fall into the trap of buying, updating, and perfecting your technology while ignoring other aspects of your business and convincing yourself you're doing it for business reasons.

Before buying or upgrading, ask yourself, "How will this benefit my business?" If there's no clear answer—one that justifies the investment in time and money—then your investment is not a rationale one.

Advertisers and salespeople tout the latest technology offerings with such statements as "This investment in your business will pay dividends" or "Leave your competition in the dust." In some cases, these claims might be valid, but in other cases they are mere hype. If you can see the benefits and honestly believe they are worth the cost and effort, the investment may be worth it. Otherwise, be very careful.

In Chapter 9, I discussed the concept of overhead and cautioned about its danger to lifestyle businesses. Overhead tends to take away the lifestyle entrepreneur's freedom because it demands constant servicing (read paying money). The lower your overhead, the freer you are to pursue activities other than running your company. If you go into debt to buy lots of technology, that debt has to be paid. If the technology allows you to pay the debt (and then some) without taking your time away from other chosen pursuits, it's probably a good investment. If it forces you to work more hours than you want or do things you don't want to just to pay for it, it's probably a bad investment.

The New Self-Employment Infrastructure

In the past 20 years, a whole ad hoc infrastructure that supports very small businesses has taken root. Though it developed without the fanfare of gee-whiz technology, it is no less a lifestyle entrepreneurship enabler. In the not-too-distant past, many of the nuts-and-bolts resources that are all but essential to virtually all businesses were available only through *real* offices. Now anyone (with the possible exception of people living in remote communities) has ready access to these essential resources. Even if, for example, you don't have your own copy machine, copy centers abound that can provide everything from single black and white copies to bound color presentations. Overnight delivery services mean that just about anyone can get just about anything to clients just about anywhere very quickly. Although basic office supplies have been generally available for a long time, the selection that superstores like Staples and Office Depot offer has not. You could buy pens and typing paper from the local stationery or drug store, but you couldn't so easily buy presentation binders, overhead projectors, or transparencies. Office superstores have done a lot to make self-employment practical.

Traditional offices were once the only respectable venue for a business meeting, but now Starbucks and coffee shops of similar ilk are acceptable meeting places. Some Starbucks even offer Internet access, and all offer a reasonably comfortable atmosphere for a client meeting for the price of a couple of cups of premium coffee.

Even the camaraderie offered by office coworkers can be partly replaced by the associations and organizations popping up as meeting places for entrepreneurs looking for affiliation with their peers. Given the increasing numbers of people choosing to go out on their own, even more resources and services catering to the self-employed are sure to develop.

Leaving a job in favor of small business or self-employment was difficult in the past and remains difficult today. However, the tools that modern technology offers as well as the entire supporting infrastructure make certain practical issues easier to deal with.

CHAPTER

12

Special Issues of Home Business

In the not-too-distant past, working at home often meant not really working or perhaps keeping busy between jobs. Serious businesses were simply not located in spare bedrooms. This attitude has changed a great deal over the last ten years or so. Today, working at home is fashionable, and many of those who can't do it are envious of those who can.

Fashionable or not, a home-based business is no longer a rarity. Daniel Pink, in his book *Free Agent Nation* (Warner Books, 2001) noted the following:

- A Wells Fargo study found that 69 percent of all new businesses are located in the owner's residence.
- The American Association of Home Based Businesses estimated that in 2001 there were more than 24 million home businesses in the United States.
- The business group IDC estimates that there were over 37 million home-based businesses in 2002.

Whether the actual number is 24 million or 37 million or somewhere in between, the trend is clearly upward. If you plan to work from home, suffice it to say you are not alone.

As I discussed in the previous chapter, technology and other enablers have been partially responsible for making home business possible, but I think shifting attitudes toward the structure and definition of work has played a part as well.

A lifestyle business does not have to be located in the home, but many are. It certainly saves on overhead when compared with renting office space, and it eliminates commuting time. For some lifestyle entrepreneurs, the ability to spend time at home is the driving force for setting up a business in the first place. This would be the case, for example, for those who want to spend time caring for their small children.

Obviously, basing a business in the home is more appropriate for some kinds of businesses than for others. For walk-in retailing (as opposed to Web-based or mail order), a home-based business is quite out of the question as it is for most types of manufacturing and most businesses that need lots of inventory or heavy equipment. But for many types of personal services, Web-based businesses, or businesses conducted largely by telephone, working from home is quite practical.

From someone who has worked primarily from home for the past 15 years, following are several issues to consider.

Separating Work Life from Home Life

Perhaps the biggest complaint I hear from home workers is that it's difficult to separate work from household responsibilities. The dishes in the sink or the faucet that needs fixing can be easily ignored from an office five miles away, but it may be difficult to ignore them from home. Home workers face dozens of distractions, ranging from housekeeping to social events to easy access to a refrigerator.

It's important to discipline yourself to put aside household issues when it's work time. I find, as do others I talk with, that it is easier to put aside household distractions when you have a clearly separate workspace. If you can close yourself in an office and get into a working mentality, the dishes in the sink and the faucet that needs a new washer seem pretty far away (though in my case the refrigerator sometimes doesn't).

Tax Deductibility

Another advantage of home-based businesses is the tax breaks. The rules are strict, but they are completely legal if you meet the tests for home office deductibility. By all means, talk to your accountant about this to make sure you follow the rules and that you reap all the benefits you're due. These are some of the general rules:

- The area you use for business must be completely for business. If you claim the entire third floor of your house is for business, technically that means no other activities are taking place on the third floor. The area that is set aside for business use is deductible as a business expense based on the percentage of the house that it occupies. If you use 25 percent of your house entirely for business, then 25 percent of your mortgage payments, electric bill, water bill, and so on could be legally classified as business expenses and therefore deductible from your taxable income.
- The space you use at home must be essential to the operation of your business. If, for example, you restore antique cars and rent a garage with no office space, it is fair to say that a home office is essential for sending bills, bookkeeping, and the like. If, on the other hand, that garage has a modern office attached to it, the IRS may well decide that you don't need an office in your home and therefore might not allow a home office deduction.

Again, check with your accountant to make sure you are eligible or can become eligible for potentially valuable home office deductions.

Outdated Laws

Years ago, municipal laws were established in many communities to prohibit working from home. The purpose was to keep residential neighborhoods . . . well, residential, unspoiled by the noise and traffic of industry and commerce. To a large degree, the purpose of those laws is antiquated. When they were made, there were no home computers or fax machines that made it possible to operate many types of businesses from home without being unneighborly.

The bad news is that those antiquated laws are still on the books in many places. The good news is they are rarely enforced unless someone files a complaint. In some places, working at home is permissible; in other places, it is permissible only with an official variance from the municipality; and in some places, it is permissible for some kinds of businesses but not for others.

In my own town, working at home is prohibited except for certain medical doctors and attorneys (no, there isn't any particular logic to those professions being favored). Yet I've been working at home for most of my workweek for many years, as have many other people I know in the same town. My neighbors know I work at home and are actually happy about it, figuring that at least one adult is around in the event of an emergency. If you plan to work at home, you might want to check on the law and its enforcement with your lawyer or with the municipal zoning authorities.

Insurance Issues

Insurance is an important issue for home workers. Your homeowners or renters insurance probably excludes home businesses from coverage, which means that if any business equipment is stolen or destroyed, you won't be reimbursed unless you have a business rider or a separate business policy. More important, if someone in your house on business—customer, employee, or anyone else—is injured, you may not be covered for liability, meaning that you may be personally liable.

Insurance rates and even eligibility for coverage are determined largely by the type of business you're operating. In general, for most kinds of lifestyle businesses, additional coverage for a home business is not very expensive. Check with your insurance agent about coverage.

Summary

Many lifestyle businesses are home-based businesses. As technology and cultural perceptions advance, working at home is an increasingly viable and popular option. Even though it is appropriate for many lifestyle businesses, it is not appropriate for those who rely on frequent client or customer visits or on any but very light business equipment. Working from home is technically prohibited in some localities, but these antiquated regulations are seldom strictly enforced.

CHAPTER

13

Negotiating and Protecting Yourself

Too often, small business people suffer an undeserved inferiority complex when it comes to negotiating, making deals, and handling disputes. They assume that the other side holds all the power. Larger companies, the thinking goes, have the clout that size and money bring, and any customer has the power to take his business elsewhere. Clients and customers make the rules; as a mere self-employed entrepreneur, you follow their rules for fear they'll find someone who will if you won't.

Too many small entrepreneurs enter a negotiation exuding a subservient position—"leading with your chin," I call it. They are saying, if not with words but with body language and mannerisms, "Please, sir, I'll accept anything you offer me, because I don't believe I have a choice." They assume they have little, if any, negotiating leeway, and trying to negotiate might ruin everything.

It's often said, however, that everything is negotiable—it's true. Some things are more negotiable than others to be sure; and even when something is said to be nonnegotiable, assume it's negotiable anyway, because it probably is.

If someone is taking the time and effort to discuss a business arrangement or resolve a dispute with you, you have some power.

If you didn't, the other party wouldn't be interested in talking to you in the first place. Sometimes, the only way to determine just how much power you have in a situation is to test it—that is, try negotiating a better deal for yourself and see whether you get a yes, a no, a maybe, or a counteroffer.

To negotiate effectively, you must have a sense of how important making a deal or reaching a resolution is to the other side. Ignore the bluster, the threats, and the warnings that it's the final offer or it's not negotiable. Pay attention to the reaction when the other party perceives the deal to be in danger of collapsing. Seldom will the other party say, "I have to make this deal" or "My boss will kill me if we can't come to terms here." To sense how important a deal is to the other side, you may well need to threaten to walk away if you don't get something closer to what you want. By threatening to walk away, you're taking a risk. The other side may tell you to go ahead and walk away, but before you do, understand and quantify the risk you're taking. Don't take it unless you can afford to make good on it, because you just may have to.

My friend Dave (see the third entrepreneur profile in Chapter 1) once taught a few courses at a private school, one in Latin and one in computer science. The head of the school called him in one day to ask if Dave might be interested in teaching a few more courses in each subject, offering Dave a pay rate that was the top of the scale for part-time teachers.

Dave was ambivalent whether he wanted to teach more classes. When he asked me what I thought, I advised him to decide at what price it would be worth it to him. I told him that because he was invited to teach and offered the top of the pay scale, the school must really need him; because he was ambivalent about taking on the added teaching, he had nothing to lose by asking for more pay.

He took my advice, deciding that he could threaten to walk away entirely given his ambivalence. He went to the head of the school with a confident, take-it-or-leave-it attitude (far from the subservient attitude the school head was accustomed to when negotiating with part-time teachers). At first, the school head feigned shock at Dave's gall in asking for 30 percent more than the maximum. But when Dave made clear he would walk away, somehow the school head found enough money to negotiate (to about 20 percent over the stated maximum).

It turned out well for Dave, but he was taking a calculated risk. The head of the school could have told him to leave and probably would have if a large pool of Latin and computer teachers were available. It was worth the risk given the indication that the school needed him and that Dave wouldn't have been too upset if the head had said no.

The biggest disadvantage lifestyle entrepreneurs face is their lack of negotiating experience. Managers and executives of large companies have often had considerable experience in business negotiation. The guy at the other end of the table may know how to bluff, bluster, and even intimidate. But if he needs what you have to offer, he doesn't hold all the cards. He may be under pressure from his boss to make a deal without wasting time talking to lots of potential suppliers for the service you're offering.

No matter how much experience the negotiating parties have, many things are said that needn't be taken literally. The problem: you won't necessarily know what should or shouldn't be taken at face value. Once again, you have to test. For example, suppose you're offering to do a certain job for $2,000 and the person to whom you're making the offer tells you someone else offered to do it for $1,000. His hope, obviously, is that you'll lower your price. You might, however, take a risk and politely say, "If you have a qualified person who can do this job for $1,000, I'm afraid I can't compete with that. I would go ahead and have him do it." He might take your advice and hire that person. More likely, though, you'll discover that his statement was a half-truth—maybe your competition could do the job for $1000 but wouldn't be able to start for three months, or maybe his work is less than competent, or maybe he can do *some* of the job for $1,000. Bluster and half-truths are part of negotiating as is taking the risk of calling the other guy's bluff–with tact and politeness of course.

Experienced negotiators don't take negotiations personally, and neither should you. The bluster and bluffing and in fact the whole process is sometimes seen as a game. At the end of the game, the players usually shake hands and silently agree to forget about some of the things that may have been said. Professional negotiators can battle all day with threats and bluffs, then go out and have a drink together after the deal is signed.

Negotiating with Yourself

In my business brokering work, prospective buyers often ask sellers something like this: "All right, you're asking $800,000 for your company, but no one ever gets their asking price. How much would you really take?" I always warn sellers beforehand not to answer this question. Rather, invite the buyer to make his offer and then respond to it. To lower your asking price or to change your terms without an offer from the other guy is negotiating with yourself. If you already made an offer or a proposal, you are much better served by inviting the other side to respond to it.

In the case of the $800,000 business, if the seller says, "All right, I'll go to $700,000," before the buyer says anything, the starting point of negotiation was just lowered. It's better to let the buyer in this case offer $500,000 and then let the seller respond. When both parties are participating, it's a negotiation; when only one side is participating, it's merely a giveaway.

Self-Protection

If push comes to shove, you need the power to shove back. You need leverage to defend your position; the moral high ground or the sureness that you are right doesn't provide enough leverage. You need something more, something like a strong contract, partial payment already in your hands, or a product or service not fully delivered to the client. I'm not talking about getting the job or making the sale in the first place. I'm talking instead about such issues as getting paid what you're owed or resolving the kinds of disputes and misunderstandings that come up in business from time to time.

In the vast majority of cases, the product or service is delivered, and the customer is happy—or at least satisfied—and pays the agreed amount within a reasonable period. If this weren't the case, business couldn't be done the way it is—we'd be constantly arguing and litigating. I'm also not talking about relatively small amounts of money. There are times when customers return merchandise for no obvious reason, times when customers don't pay you without cause, and times when collecting a debt costs more than the unpaid amount. Protection against all these possible eventualities is probably impossible and definitely not worth the cost and effort.

If, for example, you're teaching clarinet for $30 per lesson, elaborate contracts or other protection is probably not worth the cost and effort. Perhaps a policy of not teaching more than three lessons without payment is all the protection you need; your total exposure is only $90, not enough to justify a lot of expense or effort in self-protection.

A few years ago, I made a deal with a small company to do follow-up telephoning for me. I agreed to pay a total of $400, with half paid up front and the balance due net 30 days of the job completion. The next day the owner of the company presented me with a three-page contract. Although about half of it was boilerplate, she had to have spent at least an hour personalizing and modifying it for our little deal. I agreed to sign the contract, though I also advised her that I thought she was wasting a lot of effort by creating elaborate contracts for jobs of this size. Her whole risk was $200, as I was paying half before the job started. If I didn't pay, her only real option would have been to sue me in small claims court, which would cost $40 just to file.

She would then have to appear in court, probably wait for hours, and, if successful, she would then have to collect the money owed her. Given that the risk was small and that she was dealing with an established company, why bother with an elaborate contract?

With bigger projects, though, you need more protection—some leverage just in case. If you're developing a $10,000 Web site for a client, the prospect of not getting paid for your work is decidedly unpleasant. Even the possibility of having to spend several days on modification based on your client's whimsical change of approach is a situation worth avoiding. Once again, there are no 100 percent guarantees, but there are steps you can take to minimize your risk.

A little earlier I noted that the vast majority of business deals are successfully consummated and paid for without serious disagreement. What might seem a contradiction is that when entering into a big-ticket business deal, assume that if people can avoid paying you, they will. This may sound not only like a contradiction but also like paranoia, because most people feel morally obligated to pay for goods and services they receive. However, you don't want to fully rely on others' interpretation of morality; it may not be the same as yours and may be subject to situational justification if the amount of money is large enough.

In most states, you need a license to broker the sale of real estate. Any real estate broker will tell you that the lawyer for the party responsible for the commission will ask to see the broker's license just before the closing. If the broker doesn't have a license, the lawyer may well advise his client that he does not legally have to pay the broker, regardless of how good a job the broker may have done. The lawyer and his client may not agree, but from the broker's perspective, he was cheated out of the commission to which he was *morally* entitled.

Lawyers look for words and phrases in agreements that can offer their clients ways to weasel out of agreements in whole or in part. A lawyer gains points with her client and doing the job she is hired to do by finding seemingly inconsequential phrases that can be interpreted in ways that put her client in a superior negotiating position. If a lawyer finds a loophole that favors her client but thinks it is morally wrong (based on her morality) to capitalize on it and therefore does not point out the loophole to her client, she is not doing her job.

How can you minimize your risk and gain leverage just in case you have to? Of a number of possibilities, following are some of the more common ways to minimize your risk.

Try to Obtain a Credit Check

Our system of doing business is based largely on faith that people will meet their obligations to deliver the product they agree to deliver, provide the service they agree to provide, and pay for the product or service they agree to pay for. Because faith is an imperfect guarantee, a few very large companies thrive by procuring information about how well companies and individuals honor their agreements and fulfill their obligations. Credit bureaus like Equifax, TransUnion and Experian collect information about the bill-paying histories of individuals and translate those histories into credit ratings. Other organizations—the best known is Dun & Bradstreet (D&B)—do essentially the same thing for businesses.

Unfortunately, smaller companies don't have ready access to individual credit reports. Such information is generally available by subscription, and those subscriptions are purposely priced to be affordable by banks and large businesses, not by lifestyle entrepreneurs. However, your banker might check a credit file for you (especially if you owe that bank money, and your financial well-being is in its interest). The Internet may someday offer more direct access to personal credit information for smaller companies. The technology is available to be sure, but issues of privacy are obstacles to easier access to personal credit information.

Credit information for businesses is easier to obtain. Anyone can buy a D&B report, though they can be pricey. For current rates and further information check D&B's Web site at <www.dnb.com>.

A few credit reporting services now sell limited credit reports less expensively than does D&B. The amount of information is considerably less than you receive from a full-fledged D&B report, but it may be enough to make credit-granting decisions. One supplier of stripped-down credit information is InfoUsa at <www.infousa.com>.

Insist on a Signed Contract

A contract is simply an agreement between two people or entities that need not be written in all cases—generally, a verbal agreement is a legal contract. If a contract is not in writing, however, it is possible that different parties to the contract will have different recollections and interpretations as to what was said and what was agreed to. If there is a disagreement, you are far better protected by a written contract than an oral one (providing, of course, that a written contract backs your position).

Unfortunately, legalese and plain English are not always the same. Words have very specific technical meanings in contracts and are not always the meaning that nonlawyers would expect. For this reason, I advise you to seek a lawyer's advice in developing a contract. Unless you are dealing with big-ticket items, you probably don't need your lawyer to create a new contract each time you need one. Rather, get your lawyer to assist you in creating a template contract that can be modified for various (related) situations.

A signed contract minimizes serious disputes simply because the expectations and requirements for the signing parties are clearly spelled out. If disputes do arise, they can often be settled by carefully reading the contract. In the unlikely event that you end up in litigation, the outcome will be largely determined by the specifics of the contract, not by who threatens more or who feels more morally justified.

Finally, consider a clause in your contract that commits both parties to settle based on binding arbitration. Binding arbitration essentially takes the contract's interpretation out of the court's hands and puts it in the hands of an objective arbitrator, typically cheaper, quicker, and arguably fairer than a formal court confrontation. Ask your lawyer about the wisdom of using a binding arbitration clause in your situation.

Consider Up-Front and Progress Payments

Get paid as much as you can as soon as you can. It may sound crass, but it's hard to find a better lever than money in hand. Suppose you agreed to create a Web site for a client, and he agreed to pay you $6,000 for your work. Further suppose you agreed that the entire amount due would be paid on completion of the project, or you made no specific stipulation for payment terms, so he reasonably assumed he would pay you on completion. The client approved of the site at several review points along the way, but now he says he doesn't like it and refuses to pay until you make lots of changes. You suspect there is some ulterior motive for the complaints and fear that even if you do make all the changes, you still won't get paid. Your position is a difficult one. You've done a lot of work and haven't been paid a dime. You're not sure whether to do more work because you fear you might still get paid nothing, although you might get paid the whole amount.

Now suppose the same situation happens with one difference. Instead of agreeing to be paid at the end of the project, you insisted on being paid one-third of the total in advance, one-third at an agreed midpoint, and the final one-third on completion. When the client signed off at the agreed second payment point, you had collected $4,000; now the worst-case scenario is that you won't be paid $2,000. This wouldn't be good, of course, but it's 66 percent better than the first scenario. Your position is further enhanced if you have full or partial control of the Web site such that your client can't readily use it without your enabling it in some way (see below).

Another point that seems too obvious to mention but isn't: you are in a better bargaining position if you have some of the client's money in your hand than if you don't.

Hold Back Delivery of Final Product

In either scenario above, you're in a weaker position if the Web site is in your client's possession. You may be able to sue and win, but in the meantime he has the Web site and you have a collection problem. Now suppose you hadn't delivered a fully working copy of the Web site. Your client is out his whole investment until you deliver the site, giving you heavy-duty leverage. Of course, under the first scenario above, if the client decided he doesn't really want the site and hasn't paid you anything—well, you're back to square one. Under the second scenario, however, assuming he wants the site, you're in a nice position of power.

You don't have to withhold delivery entirely to achieve this kind of leverage. Retaining enough to cripple the product would achieve pretty much the same objective. For example, school photographers often send out actual photos of kids when inviting parents to buy them. The only problem is that "proof" or "sample only" or a similar phrase is written across the photo to assure that you can't use the photo without paying for it.

Know the Legalities

Knowledge is power. You need to know the legalities that apply to your profession or industry and the customary interpretation of those legalities in your field. If you design Web sites, for example, you have to know about using other people's materials and who owns the design of the finished site. If you're a freelance writer, what happens if you sell a story to a magazine and then another magazine wants the same story with additions and changes?

Are you free to sell rights to that second magazine? Of course, if you have a contract that spells this out, it's easy to answer. But what if you have no contract?

Professional associations are a good place for learning the basic legal issues in a given field or industry. Some of the large associations have lawyers on staff or retainer and often have booklets that explain the more common legal issues. Even a smaller organization may be able to refer you to lawyers familiar with the field it represents.

Self-Serving Letters

Have you ever received a letter from a company that did little more than state the obvious? Perhaps it was in the form of a thank-you: "Thank you for permitting ABC Appliance Repair to repair your dryer. We're glad it is now working properly." Or perhaps it was a letter filled with legalese confirming your airline reservation and flight times with an explanation of cancellation penalties. Letters like these are designed to give the sender leverage if a later dispute arises. Although you still may be able to claim your dryer doesn't work properly, ABC Appliance Repair gained a bit of leverage if you don't respond to the thank-you letter.

Suppose you're a Web site designer, and a client is reviewing progress along the way; sending that client a letter with language like the following could be helpful in protecting you from the client's decision at the end of the project that he wants a totally different kind of site:

"Thanks for taking the time to review our work on your Web site to date. I'm glad you are happy with our work to date. Please let me know immediately if there are any problems or suggestions. As we discussed at our meeting, we will continue with the design format that we agreed to at the beginning of this project."

Keep Copies of Documents

You never know which document you may need some day. When everything is going along fine, it may seem unnecessary to carefully file contracts, letters, and notes. However, one day a seemingly unimportant document may suddenly become essential to prove that you did have the customer's approval of the completed job, that you did bill the client in a timely manner, or that you did indeed have a written agreement in the first place.

When push comes to shove, it is hard to overestimate the value of paper documentation to support your claim. Judges and arbitrators don't have the information about what was agreed to or what was implied verbally; they rely largely on printed documents. Even parties to agreements don't remember clearly what they may have agreed to, and there is nothing like a printed document to refresh one's memory.

The Art of Threatening Legal (or Other) Action

As I've already said, only a tiny proportion of business agreements end up in court or arbitration. It is even true that only a small fraction of serious disagreements end up in court or arbitration. Far more often than not, disagreements are amicably settled through a mix of bluster and negotiation.

Sophisticated negotiators seldom threaten legal action early on in a negotiation. They may, however, gently imply that they are prepared to take things further: "I'm hoping we can work this out without the expense of a legal confrontation." A statement like that gets the attention of the other party without arousing defensiveness or intransigence. Legal action and arbitration should be seen as a last resort, as it is almost always better for everyone if a disagreement can be settled between the parties. However, the more leverage you have, the better the settlement you will be able to negotiate.

Don't Be Afraid of Bigness

Small business owners, freelancers, and other entrepreneurs tend to be intimidated by large companies, whose executives understand this tendency and often play the intimidation factor to the hilt. They like to convey this type of message: "We're ABC, Inc., a company with sales of 4 billion dollars and influence with senators, governors, and the Pope. You can't challenge us! We make the rules; you follow them or we crush you."

Well, even if they do have influence with the Pope, chances are they're not going to call in a favor on what to them is a small issue. Chances are that even if you are having a dispute with, say, their art director over the Web site you designed, and the art director is angry and would, if he could, bring all the corporate resources to bear against you, he won't be able to. Large companies make decisions based on business logic. Even though they may well have lots of legal resources at their disposal, you, in fact, have some David advantages over Goliath. First, it will likely be far cheaper for a large company to reach an amicable settlement with you than to get involved in a court or arbitration battle. Even if a situation did get as far as court, unless several thousand dollars were at stake, chances are the company would assign the case to a young, inexperienced lawyer, not its top litigators, thereby evening the playing field.

If you're operating as a proprietorship, in most states you can sue in small claims court if only small amounts are involved. In most states, you can represent yourself, but your large corporate adversary would have to send a lawyer, making it more economical for you to fight than for the corporation to.

Big companies hate bad press, and any story about the little guy facing off against a big company is bad press for the big company, no matter how legally defensible its position may be. A viable publicity threat may beat a legal threat in getting that big company to settle things in your favor.

Finally, if you're not happy with the corporate person with whom you're dealing, you can go over her head to her boss, her boss's boss, and so on up the ladder. Corporate employees hate it when someone goes over their head, so you can use this threat as a lever. You own your company so they can't threaten to go over your head (one of the really nice things about being your own boss).

Several years ago, my video company completed what to us was a large job for a large museum, which had received a grant of about $75,000 for the video. The client loved the finished product, signed off on it but didn't send our final $25,000 payment in the 30 days as stipulated in our agreement. After 40 days, I sent the museum a polite letter requesting payment; after 50 days, I called to ask for payment but received only this response: "You'll be paid soon; stop bothering us." After 70 days, I sent a letter demanding payment and threatening legal action in a polite way, of course. I also sent a copy of that letter with a copy of the contract itself, the original invoice, and the form with the client's signature accepting the final video to the chairman of the foundation that granted the $75,000 for the video in the first place. I included a brief cover letter with the sentence, "Is there anything you can do to avoid the expense and unplesantries of a legal confrontation?"

The chairman of the foundation never responded to me, but the museum certainly did. Four days after the letter was sent, I received a call from the museum's chief financial officer apologizing for the late payment and promising we would have a check within a week. We did.

Winning the Battle, Losing the War

This is a cautionary note against using even polite and veiled threats to a client. Understand that you are taking a risk of alienating that client, so you have to calculate how far to push. To make this calculation, consider the downside: how much you have to lose if you do alienate that client. If you have no likelihood of future business, the risk is probably worth it. If we're talking about a long-term client, be more careful.

My museum example above was a one-time job with no likelihood that we would be doing another job for that organization. The people with whom we worked directly, I'm sure, were livid that we went over their heads to the foundation, but that didn't concern me too much. If this had been, or was likely to become, a regular client, I probably would have made a different calculation and waited longer before taking that drastic step.

In another personal example, we also had a regular client who was uncharacteristically late in paying us a large fee. He needed the master videotape that we held and that my partner and I decided was our major leverage. We agonized over what to do—withhold the tape and risk alienating a good client who was late in paying us versus releasing the tape in the hope that we would get paid and retain the client's goodwill. The ending wasn't quite so happy for us in this case. We decided to play hardball and withhold the master tape. We did get paid after telling him our intent, but we also lost a very good client. Perhaps he was just temporarily short of cash, and we would have gotten paid anyway and retained his business; or perhaps we wouldn't have gotten any future business from him *and* we wouldn't have gotten paid if we hadn't withheld the tape. Who knows? We made the best decision we could with the information available at the time, and we'll never know what would have been.

Deciding between taking or threatening action and avoiding it to retain goodwill is seldom an easy one. I can offer no universal advice because situations differ as do the personalities involved. My best advice is to think through the pros, cons, and risks involved in view of the possible outcomes and the likelihood of each outcome. Base your decision on rational calculations more than on the emotion of the situation.

Summary

Although it may not always be labeled as such, negotiating is a part of business. You may be regularly negotiating price and terms with a prospective client. Or you, as the buyer, may be negotiating with suppliers to your business or with a banker on loan terms. Because negotiating is such a common business occurrence, learning how to do it effectively will prove quite helpful.

Lesson number one: Don't go into a negotiation assuming a subservient position. Unfortunately, too many small business people assume the other party holds the power and accept subservience as their only alternative. If someone wants something that you can supply, you have certain power in the situation.

Closely related to the concept of business negotiation is the concept of self-protection. You need to minimize the likelihood that you'll be cheated in some way. This involves taking steps to protect yourself and knowing how to negotiate your way through occasional confrontations. Most business deals work out fine. Sometimes small misunderstandings, disagreements, and jockeying for position crop up, but most differences are amicably ironed out without the threat of lawsuits and the like. If this weren't the case, business would be nothing but constant fights and lawsuits.

When the occasional problems do come up, you should be prepared to handle them and you should have some leverage on your side. The better prepared you are when going into a confrontation, the more leverage you have; and the better you are at negotiating, the more likely the differences will be settled in your favor.

CHAPTER

14

Health Insurance

A complete discussion of health insurance is beyond the scope of this book. Let's just say that we currently have a complex problem with health insurance in this country that probably won't be alleviated for quite awhile. This problem, with its inherent complexities, is a particularly important issue for lifestyle entrepreneurs and small business owners. Employees of large organizations are generally wholly or partly covered through their employer via group policies negotiated and arranged by their employer. Self-employed people, small business owners, and employees of small business often have difficulty in getting quality coverage and are likely to pay higher rates than do employees of large organizations.

A number of would-be entrepreneurs avoid graduating to self-employment simply because of fears about obtaining health insurance. For many people, the prospect of forgoing a regular paycheck is less frightening than the prospect of forgoing health insurance. With medical costs for catastrophic (and even less-than-catastrophic) illness being what they are, health insurance is essential. I say that not only as a small business person but also as a cancer survivor who has had to rely on that coverage in a major way. It is not an exaggeration to say that you are not only risking financial ruin if you go without coverage but such coverage can literally mean the difference between life and death.

Even though health insurance is an issue to contend with in taking the plunge to self-employment, it is not an insurmountable obstacle. The basic difficulty is that health insurers prefer to insure larger groups. It is cheaper on a per-insured basis to administer a plan for 2,000 people than for one self-employed person. Also, rates are based largely on the insurer's risk assessment for the entire group. A very small group with one person who has a serious health problem (serious being defined as expensive or potentially expensive for the insurer) pays extremely high rates. However, if that same person is part of a large group and becomes part of a statistically small percentage of people in the group with serious health conditions, the cost to the insurer is spread over the entire group and is therefore less of an issue.

The situation, though, isn't hopeless for entrepreneurs. Many self-employed people have reasonable medical coverage at reasonable rates. This is possible in virtually all cases through some sort of group affiliation where rates (premiums) are set for the group as a whole and apply to all members of that group.

The following sections explain some of the ways in which self-employed people and small business owners can obtain health insurance.

Coverage through spouse. Sometimes, it's this simple. If your spouse has coverage through his or her employer (or through any other channel), you should be all set. If your spouse is entitled to coverage but you haven't been taking advantage of that coverage because his or her employer pays only for the employee (not the entire family), now is the time to pay whatever you're required to pay to upgrade to family coverage. Opting in to a large employer's plan is likely to be a better deal, probably better coverage with fewer restrictions than you'll get through any of your other options. Even if your spouse isn't planning to stay at his or her job for the long term, this may still be the way to go for now. Coverage can likely be extended beyond the end of your spouse's tenure at that job through COBRA (see below).

COBRA (Consolidated Omnibus Budget Reconciliation Act). This federal law, instituted in 1985, essentially requires most employers to allow employees who terminate voluntarily or are terminated for any reason other than "gross misconduct" to continue coverage through that employer's plan. You have to pay into that plan at the rate the employer pays, probably with a small surcharge to cover administrative expenses. Generally, your employer must allow you to continue to buy into the plan for up to 18 months after termination. Employers of fewer than 20 (including part-time workers) are exempt from COBRA.

Some states have their own "mini-COBRA" laws that extend the federal minimums. Check with your state's commissioner of insurance or your lawyer.

For more details on the ins and outs of COBRA, take a look at <www.insure.com/health/cobra.html>. In fact, the <www.insure.com> Web site has a lot of great information about health insurance for self-employed people and small businesses.

Professional associations. Some trade and professional associations offer group health insurance policies to their members. As discussed above, group coverage rates are based on health and age characteristics of the group as a whole. In general, all eligible members of the group can purchase insurance coverage under the plan without regard to physical condition.

Chamber of commerce and other business organizations. When you become self-employed or start a small business you gain a new professional designation: businessperson. As such, you can join organizations such as your local chamber of commerce. Many chambers of commerce and other business organizations have negotiated group plans with insurance providers and can offer coverage to members. Many lifestyle entrepreneur's join their local chamber primarily to obtain this group health insurance.

National Association for the Self-Employed. The primary purpose of this organization is to make health insurance available to self-employed people and small business owners, although it has branched into other types of insurance and noninsurance products. It tends to use high-pressure selling tactics and, in my experience, tends to be a bit cagey about what is covered under what circumstances. It is worth talking to, but compare its offerings to others in terms of cost and coverage. Its Web site is <www.nase.org>.

Group coverage for your business. In 1996, the Health Insurance Portability and Accountability Act became law. It included a number of provisions that make access to health insurance a bit easier for consumers. One of the provisions that directly affects small business mandates that health insurance companies servicing small groups must accept every small employer that applies for coverage; however, it generally defines small employer as a company that employs at least two people. As a result, group coverage may be available to your business at some cost. In all likelihood it will be more expensive than a policy through a larger group, especially if you are older, if you or a family member have a preexisting condition, or if you are judged to be a higher risk for any reason.

Military service. Active duty and retired uniformed military personnel and their families and survivors of all uniformed services members who are not eligible for Medicare are eligible for the military's medical insurance program called Tricare. The program is free for active duty personnel, but there are some charges for nonactive duty personnel who use the Tricare option. See the Web site for more information at <tricare.osd.mil>, or talk to your local Veterans Affairs officer.

Medical savings accounts (MSA). By the time this book goes to press, MSAs may or may not exist because they are set to be reevaluated by Congress in the current year. An MSA is a tax-exempt trust or custodial account with a financial institution (a bank or an insurance company) in which you can save money for future medical expenses.

MSAs are currently available only to small employers and the self-employed. A small employer is defined as one who has an average of 50 or fewer employees during either of the last two calendar years. A new employer is also considered a small employer for MSAs if he or she reasonably expects to employ 50 or fewer people in the current year.

MSAs are not designed to replace health insurance. Rather, they are designed to help pay medical expenses for those who have high deductible health plans (which many lower-cost plans are). In fact, they are available only to people who have high deductible health plans. If you have, or plan to get, a high deductible health plan, you may want to look into MSAs as a tax-advantaged way to save for the eventuality of major out-of-pocket health expenses.

MSA rules are currently explained on a Medicare Web page: <www.medicare.gov/publications/pubs/nonpdf/msa.asp>.

Tax deductibility of health insurance. C corporations (see Chapter 7) have always been able to pay 100 percent of the cost of health insurance for their employees (including their owner, if that owner was an employee) as a deductible business expense. Before 2003, however, S corporations and unincorporated self-employed persons could deduct only part of the cost of such insurance. The law changed in 2003 so that now all business entities can deduct the full cost of health insurance for their employees, including employee-owners.

Summary

Health insurance is justifiably a major concern of people in their own business and those planning to take the entrepreneurial plunge. Scare stories about self-employed people being denied access to coverage abound. Some of these scare stories may be true, but the situation is better than it was a few years ago. Although getting insurance may be a bit difficult and expensive for the self-employed, it is obtainable.

If your spouse is covered under a large group plan and you can get coverage through his or her plan, that is probably your best option even if there is a charge. Failing that, your next best bet is to become part of a group that has group rate coverage for its members, such as a professional association or a business group like a chamber of commerce.

COBRA (Consolidated Omnibus Budget Reconciliation Act) provides a temporary stopgap alternative (typically 18 months) by compelling employers (other than small organization employers) at the employees' expense to continue terminated employees under its group plan.

CHAPTER

15

Common Mistakes, Myths, and Misconceptions of Lifestyle Entrepreneurs

Throughout my years of consulting with small business owners and self-employed people, I have seen mistakes being made and heard myths and misconceptions about small business management presented as gospel truth. And, yes, I'll admit it, I made my share of business mistakes along the way. An old saying admonishes us to learn from our mistakes. This is certainly good advice, but wouldn't it be better still if we could learn from the mistakes of others before we make them ourselves? To some degree, we can.

There are enough small business mistakes to fill an entire book; I know this because I wrote that book ten years ago (*How to Avoid 101 Small Business Mistakes, Myths, and Misconceptions.* The Consultant Press, NY, 1991). This chapter outlines some of the most common mistakes I've seen and myths held out as business truths specifically among the self-employed and lifestyle entrepreneurs.

My Product Is So Good, Customers Will Beat a Path to My Door

Perhaps at one time a superior product would sell well solely because it *was* superior, and a superior practitioner would be certain to gain the most clients because of his superior skills. But in today's marketplace, intrinsic product or service quality is only one of the factors that determine who gets the business. Even the best products and best practitioners will fail without effective marketing.

Some practitioners (in just about every field) go into their own business largely because they are very good in their chosen field. Perhaps they have won awards and accolades and reason that their skill will get them lots of clients; after all, it got them the recognition of their peers and earned them their professional reputation. Undoubtedly, skill and reputation help, but skill, reputation, and quality are only part of the marketing mix; the rest is price, promotion, and distribution.

An inferior product with strong promotion and distribution may well prevail over a superior product with weak promotion and distribution. Buyers don't always have the resources or inclination to objectively weigh products against one another and base a buying decision solely on intrinsic merit.

Further, the criteria for judging professional skills within a profession may be very different from the criteria used by consumers of that profession. Even though a cardiologist may be esteemed by other cardiologists for his technical skills, he will be judged by his patients, at least partly, on his bedside manner and his ability and willingness to explain things to patients. Likewise, an accomplished pianist who decides to teach piano to young children will be judged in part by her ability to relate to kids.

I'm not implying that quality doesn't matter; it absolutely does. But quality is judged in different ways. So far as your business is concerned, you have to be particularly sensitive to the criteria your target market uses to judge quality. Further, keep in mind that the product or service itself is only one component of the marketing mix.

If I Advertise, I'll Certainly Get a Lot More Business

I often hear new entrepreneurs reason like this: "Gee, if I'm getting ten clients a week based on word of mouth, I'll certainly get twice that many if I advertise." Marketing in general is essential, but advertising in and of itself is not always an efficient way to get more business. This logic is like saying that if two of these antibiotics a day are making me better slowly, I'll get better twice as fast if I take four a day.

Word of mouth is the best form of advertising there is. In fact, a lot of advertising is designed to initiate word of mouth. Because consumers know that paid ads are just that—paid ads—they view them with an understandable degree of healthy skepticism. A recommendation from a friend or colleague, is readily trusted so long as the recommender is considered unbiased.

Yes, advertising can work, but it isn't magic. It has to reach the right people (your target market) with the right message and with cost-effectiveness. Paying $100 to get $50 in new business simply isn't worth it. A single ad seldom does much good; generally, an ad must be repeated several times to sink in and start working. Unfortunately, some ads don't work at all, and some work incrementally; that is, each $100 spent on advertising, for example, may bring in possibly $130 over time.

If success were as simple as running a few economical ads and seeing your sales double or triple, business would be easy for just about everyone. The reality, though, is business, and especially start-up business, takes considerable trial and error, and effort and expense, to gain a customer base. Advertising can eat up a good deal of trial and error expense.

It Takes a Year (or Some Other Specified Period) for a New Business to Start Making Money

Novice entrepreneurs often ask me how long it takes for a new business to turn the corner and start making money. Others tell me they've heard it takes a year, or six months, or two years, or some defined period for a new business to get off the ground. In reality, there is no standard period to turn that corner. Some businesses are blessed; they start making money right away. Others take years to become profitable, and some never earn money.

Established franchise operations can offer averages for how long it takes for new franchisees to become profitable. One of the reasons some entrepreneurs prefer to buy rather than start businesses is that the profitability is predictable, because projections can be based on the demonstrated financial performance of the past.

However, I suspect that few readers of this book are interested in a franchise or even an acquisition option. The point at which your business starts making money is best predicted by your own research and planning, as detailed in previous sections, and not by the silly slogans and rules of thumb that are presented as gospel.

This Isn't a Real Business

A pervasive inferiority complex exists among self-employed people, especially lifestyle entrepreneurs. Somehow, only big companies are "real" businesses, and the smaller your company, the less real it is. The minimum threshold to achieve status as a "real business" is incorporation, at least in the minds of some people.

This thinking is ludicrous. A pediatrician is a real doctor even though he deals with little people, and a computer is still a computer even if it fits in a briefcase or the palm of your hand.

Likewise, if you're providing a service or selling a product for which people are paying you, you have a business. True, you are different from a multinational corporation and more limited in what you can do. A handheld computer certainly can't do what a full-fledged server can do. By the same token, when it comes to such limited and specialized tasks as keeping appointments and addresses on your person, that handheld computer has it all over the server.

A self-employed entrepreneur would be of little good performing the kinds of operations that are more appropriate for large companies, such as generating electrical power or refining gasoline. But a multinational corporation would be of little good serving a specialized niche.

There is no reason why the concept of business should be the exclusive domain of large corporations. As this book has demonstrated, the tools of business can be used as well by individuals looking for escape from that very world and for freedom of lifestyle in general.

Pretending to Be a Big Business

This is a corollary to the above misconception that only big businesses are real businesses. Small business people often assume they have to pretend they are really much bigger businesses to be taken seriously. Somehow, it is assumed, that there are inviolate rules of etiquette and protocol that businesspeople must follow to be taken seriously. One of the unwritten rules, some think, is that you must either be a big company or convince the world that you are.

People use marvelous tricks to imply they employ dozens and occupy big offices when their only employee is themself, and their office suite is a spare bedroom. You can even buy tapes that play office sounds to use as background to fool people on the phone. Voice mail can be set with instruction to press #1 for marketing, #2 for accounts payable, #3 for tech support and so on, although pressing any number gets you to the same person—the company's owner and sole employee.

It is unnecessary to pretend to be a bigger company than you really are. It may make a difference to some people, but, for the most part, prospective clients and customers are more concerned that you can do the job at hand or your product can fill their needs.

Charging by the Hour

Employees think in terms of how much they are paid for blocks of time—how much an hour, a day, or a week. New entrepreneurs carry this system over to their business, assuming it is the best way to charge for their services, probably because it's the most familiar to them.

In reality, charging by the hour (or day, etc.) should be avoided whenever possible. Charging by the hour invites comparisons and unfair ones at that. If you quote a prospective client $120 per hour, for example, he may think, "Gee, I don't make one-third that much." People who aren't in their own business don't always understand that you take the risks and have the overhead and other expenses, so your $120 charge doesn't translate to $120 that you keep. Your prospective client may resent your hourly rate of pay, and you don't need that kind of resentment.

Charging by the hour also encourages unfair comparisons with competitors. If you propose $120 an hour and your competitor proposes $85, by initial comparison you're too expensive. Suppose, though, that you can complete the job in half the time or your quality is superior; that fact is hidden by the too-easy comparison.

When possible, quote a price based on a completed job. How long it takes to complete and how much you make or don't make from that job is your business. Your customer's or client's concern is whether your price is competitive, the quality of your work good, and your delivery on time.

Charging Based on Cost

The mistake of charging by the hour applies to services, whereas charging by cost applies primarily to products. Some small business people assume they must base their pricing on their costs. Someone may, for example, mark up everything he or she sells by 20, 50, or 100 percent. In reality, different products have different values to customers, and those values probably have little to do with your costs but more to do with the costs of competing products and perceived value.

I once did consulting for a woman who was importing gift items from Europe. She sold her products wholesale and always at a 90 percent markup. However, according to the ultimate arbiter of price, the marketplace, some of the items were worth only 50 percent above her cost whereas others were worth 300 to 400 percent more than her cost. We learned this by observing how the retailers she sold to were pricing her products for resale. Because she couldn't reconcile this anomaly with her intransigent pricing policies, she continued her 90 percent markup policy and continued to leave money on the table.

Cost is only one factor to consider in your pricing. Others have to do with your product's value to customers. Sometimes it takes trial and error plus observation to get a good handle on perceived value.

Lower Price Means More Sales

If a new doctor in town advertised "Special—Doctor's Visits $20," would you leave your own doctor who was charging the going rate of $70 a visit? Would you buy coffee from a coffee shop that was selling it for 20 cents a cup when the other shops in the area were charging more than $1?

Purchase decisions are based as much on perceptions as on empirical facts. The $20 doctor may have skills equal to the other doctors in town who are charging $70, and the 20 cent cup of coffee may be equal to the $1 cup. However, the low-priced doctor and the low-priced coffee would be approached with the same skepticism by intended consumers.

Several times I've had clients who did one form of consulting or another tell me, "I raised my prices and got even more business!" A consultant who has the nerve to charge $1,500 a day may well be perceived as a top expert simply because he has the nerve to charge that much. Another in the same field, who charges $350 a day, may well be viewed as of dubious competence (or else he would charge more, right?).

I'm not suggesting that you immediately raise your rates. I am suggesting that you incrementally experiment with higher prices and that you don't assume lower prices mean more business and higher prices mean less. Consider the principle of perceived value in your pricing.

Big Business Has All the Advantages

Self-employed people and small business owners seem to think that big companies have all the advantages. Whether we're talking about negotiating a deal, selling a product, or another aspect of business, the small guy doesn't stand a chance. Fortunately, this just isn't so.

First, big companies can't handle some business activities well. Big business is based on the concept of economies of scale; that is, taking advantage of economies and efficiencies that accompany quantity buying, mass production, and large-scale mechanization. This concept works well for commodity products and services that don't require individualization, such as banking or generating electric power. But it doesn't work well for niche products or services that have to be individualized.

Second, big businesses thrive on regimentation. They have well-honed ways of doing things, which are necessary to exploit those economies of scale on which such companies are built. Entrepreneurs, especially lifestyle entrepreneurs, conduct business based partly on their wits and their ability to find clever methods and clever solutions to problems.

I live in a college area, where Brown University and Rhode Island School of Design are right down the street. A new independent sandwich shop opened a while ago near two large college dorms. It offered free delivery within a two-mile radius but didn't seem to have delivery people milling around. When I queried the owner about this, he said, "During busy times we have a guy here to deliver. For other times, we rely on a few kids in those dorms who own bikes. When we get a delivery order, we call one of them down to do the delivery. They're happy to do it for free food and the tips they'll probably get." Imagine McDonalds or Burger King doing business like that!

Third, big businesses can't be as nimble as a small company or a self-employed person. You may be able to have a business idea over breakfast and implement it before noon, even if it's a major change in direction. A large company has layers of management, committees, precedents, and sometimes shareholders who demand explanations. For large companies, even relatively small decisions take time, and major decisions that materially change the direction of the company—well, those take lots of time.

When it comes to areas where profit depends on economies of scale, big business does have all the advantages. When the nature of the business involves servicing a small niche, individualization, or spur-of-the-moment creativity, small businesses and the self-employed can compete on at least equal footing.

This Can't Be Tax Deductible—It's Fun

The IRS doesn't care how happy or miserable you may be or whether you hate your work or love it. Some people assume that if they are enjoying something, such as a business trip, then it can't possibly be a deductible business expense. Not so. You can even mix business with pleasure as long as you deduct only the business part. If the pleasure happens to be legitimate business, it's deductible.

As a practical matter, few people that I know of refrain from deducting business expenses simply because they are enjoyable. They do, however, become overly cautious and perhaps deduct part of a business trip (when it's fully deductible) or avoid taking more trips than absolutely necessary because "it might look suspicious."

My friend Elaine (see the entrepreneur profile in Chapter 5: "Apartments in Europe") rents apartments to American tourists in Europe. She is based in the United States but takes at least one trip a year to check out new apartments, meet with European agents, take pictures, and the like. Does she look forward to the trips? Sure she does. One of her reasons for going into this business was the frequent trips to the best places in Europe. Are the trips deductible? Sure they are. It's hard to imagine how an IRS examiner would challenge these trip expenses as being anything but reasonable. Might they arouse suspicion? Perhaps, but so do lots of other things that aren't as much fun as going to Europe. So long as Elaine keeps good documentation and receipts, the IRS won't care if she enjoyed herself and did business at the same time.

Overbuying Technology

A friend of mine who travels a lot on business and is not especially computer literate called me for some computer advice. He wanted to set up an elaborate network whereby e-mails would be logged into his database, prioritized, forwarded automatically, and more. This was doable, but I asked him why he wanted to do it. He didn't have an answer except that he travels a lot and thinks this would help him become better organized.

As it turns out, Frank really needed a basic laptop computer and a cell phone (which he already had). Although some people need more computer sophistication than that, Frank couldn't explain why it would help him. I guaranteed him it would take a lot more effort, expense, and learning than it was worth.

Don't be taken in by the computer ads that make vague promises of greater productivity or new features that you can't possibly do business without. Before venturing into new hardware or software purchases, know clearly what your goals and expectations are for the new equipment. If you can't answer what it will do for you, you probably don't really need it.

Computers and related high-tech devices are important to almost every business today. As discussed in Chapter 11, they in fact enable several kinds of lifestyle businesses that simply would not be possible to run as lifestyle businesses in the predesktop computer days. What's more, for many of us (yes, myself included) they are also fun. However, there is a tendency to confuse business need with entertainment when it comes to fancy technology. My advice is to separate the two. If you want to buy more than you really need and you can afford it, go ahead. Just be careful about convincing yourself that a business need is really a fun need in disguise.

INDEX